TOEFL VOCABULARY PRACTICE ADVANTAGE+ EDITION: ESSENTIAL WORDS FOR TOEFL TEST PREPARATION WITH WORKBOOK EXERCISES

NOTE: TOEFL, TOEFL iBT, and Test of English as a Foreign Language are registered trademarks of ETS (Educational Testing Service), which is not affiliated with nor endorses this publication.

TOEFL Vocabulary Practice Advantage+ Edition: Essential Words for TOEFL Test Preparation with Workbook Exercises

© COPYRIGHT 1995, 2014. Academic Success Media © COPYRIGHT 2020. Academic Success Group.

All rights reserved. No part of this publication may be reproduced, stored in a retrieval system, or transmitted, in any form or by any means, electronic, mechanical, photocopying, recording or otherwise.

ISBN: 978-1-949282-46-7

COPYRIGHT NOTICE TO EDUCATORS: Please respect copyright law. Under no circumstances may you make copies of these materials for distribution to or use by students. Should you wish to use the materials with students, you are required to purchase a copy of this publication for each of your students.

NOTE: TOEFL, TOEFL iBT, and Test of English as a Foreign Language are registered trademarks of ETS (Educational Testing Service), which is not affiliated with nor endorses this publication.

HOW TO USE THIS PUBLICATION:

This publication contains vocabulary like you will see on the TOEFL and TOEFL iBT examinations.

The vocabulary in the book is divided into alphabetized sections, from A to Z. You should study the vocabulary in each section, paying special attention to how the words are used in the example sentences provided. You should also devote some time to studying the derivative words for each item. For optimal performance on the exam, it is advisable to try to commit the words to memory.

Once you have studied each section, you should proceed to the exercises at the end of the chapter. The exercises will provide you with further practice in utilizing the vocabulary naturally in sentences, a skill which is assessed on the exam.

You should then check your answers to the exercises by looking at the answer key provided at the end of the book.

ABBREVIATIONS USED IN THIS PUBLICATION:

adj.	adjective
adv.	adverb
ant.	antonym
der.	derivative
e.g.	example
esp.	especially
exp.	expression
id.	idiom
met.	metaphorical
n.	noun
p. part.	past participle
ph. v.	phrasal verb
sbdy	somebody
sthg	something
syn.	synonym
v.	verb

TABLE OF CONTENTS

Words beginning with "A" – Definitions and example sentences	1
Words beginning with "A" – Exercises	6
Words beginning with "B" – Definitions and example sentences	7
Words beginning with "B" – Exercises	12
Words beginning with "C" – Definitions and example sentences	13
Words beginning with "C" – Exercises	22
Words beginning with "D" – Definitions and example sentences	23
Words beginning with "D" – Exercises	29
Words beginning with "E" – Definitions and example sentences	30
Words beginning with "E" – Exercises	35
Words beginning with "F" – Definitions and example sentences	36
Words beginning with "F" – Exercises	41
Words beginning "G – H" – Definitions and example sentences	42
Words beginning with "G – H" – Exercises	47
Words beginning with "I" – Definitions and example sentences	48
Words beginning with "I" – Exercises	53
Words beginning "J – L" – Definitions and example sentences	54
Words beginning "J – L" – Exercises	58
Words beginning "M – O" – Definitions and example sentences	59
Words beginning "M – O" – Exercises	64
Words beginning with "P" – Definitions and example sentences	65
Words beginning with "P" – Exercises	71

Words beginning "Q – R" – Definitions and example sentences	72
Words beginning "Q – R" – Exercises	78
Words beginning with "S" – Definitions and example sentences	79
Words beginning with "S" – Exercises	89
Words beginning with "T" – Definitions and example sentences	90
Words beginning with "T" – Exercises	94
Words beginning "U – V" – Definitions and example sentences	95
Words beginning "U - V" – Exercises	99
Words beginning "W – Z" – Definitions and example sentences	100
Words beginning "W – Z" – Exercises	102
Answers to the exercises	103

ADVANTAGE PLUS EDITION – WORKBOOK EXERCISES

Vocabulary Practice Test 1	111
Vocabulary Practice Test 2	115
Vocabulary Practice Test 3	119
Vocabulary Practice Test 4	123
Vocabulary Practice Test 5	127
Vocabulary Practice Test 6	131
Vocabulary Practice Test 7	135
Vocabulary Practice Test 8	139
Answers to the Practice Tests	143

Words – A

Instructions: Study the words below, paying attention to their meanings as well as how they are used in the example sentences. Then complete the exercise that follows.

abashed - (adj.) embarrassed. e.g. - She is easily abashed and often turns red from embarrassment. Der. (v.) abash; (adj.) bashful.

abdomen - (n.) the part of the body between the chest and legs. e.g. - The pregnant woman's abdomen grew larger every month. Der. (adj.) abdominal.

abscond - (v.) to leave a place secretly and go into hiding with stolen money. e.g. - Jeff stole money from the company for which he was chief accountant. Later, he absconded with the funds and is currently thought to be living in Brazil.

absorb - (v.) to use up or totally command someone's attention. e.g. - He is absorbed in his studies at present and rarely has time for anything else. Der. (n.) absorbency; (adj.) absorbent.

abstemious - (adj.) refraining from indulgence in food or drink. e.g. - An abstemious lifestyle is required in order to lose weight. Der. (adv.) abstemiously.

abstinence - (n.) the action of refraining from or not participating in certain activities. Abstinence from smoking will ensure good health. Der. (v.) abstain.

accessible - (adj.) being readily available or unrestricted. e.g. - Many buildings are not accessible to people in wheelchairs. Der. (n.) access; (n.) accessibility; (v.) access.

accommodation - (n.) the provision of rooms or housing. e.g. - The accommodation in the hotel was not as advertised since the rooms didn't have air conditioning. Der. (v.) accommodate.

accompany - (v.) to go along with; (syn.) escort. e.g. - I will accompany you to dinner. I will pick you up at your house at 6:00. Der. (n.) accompaniment.

accost - (v.) to attack; to confront aggressively. e.g. - He was accosted by an attacker in the street and was badly injured.

accumulate - (v.) to increase gradually in amount or quantity. e.g. - She did not become a millionaire overnight. She accumulated her wealth over many years. Der. (n.) accumulation; (adj.) accumulative; (adv.) accumulatively.

accustomed (to) - (adj.) having become familiar with or used to certain conditions because of habit or experience. e.g. - I became accustomed to getting up early after having had a class at 8:00 this semester. Der. (v.) accustom.

acquit - (v.) to find an accused suspect not guilty of a crime in court. e.g. - The suspect was acquitted of the crime when he was found "not guilty" by the court. Der. (n.) acquittal.

acute - (adj.) sharp; in very serious condition. e.g. - She had an acute pain in her stomach and was rushed to the hospital.

adage - (n.) an expression, saying, or proverb. e.g. - My favorite adage is: Don't count your chickens before they are hatched.

adaptable - (adj.) easily accepting change. e.g. - This product is adaptable. It has 1001 different uses. Der. (n.) adaptability (v.) adapt.

adhesive - (adj.) self-sticking. e.g. - This label is adhesive. Remove the paper from the back of it and stick it on your notebook. Der. (n.) adhesiveness; (v.) adhere; (adv.) adhesively.

adjacent - (adj.) being next door or nearby. e.g. - You don't need to go far to buy bread. There is a grocery store adjacent to our house. Der. (n.) adjacency.

adjourn - (v.) to dismiss a meeting or call it to a close. e.g. - The business meeting began at 12:00 and was adjourned at 2:00.

adornment - (n.) decoration or beautification. e.g. - Her wedding dress was decorated with many adornments. Der. (v.) adorn.

advent (of) - (n.) arrival; coming into use or existence. e.g. - The advent of the new computer system means that the old system will be disposed of.

adversary - (n.) enemy, opponent, or antagonist. e.g. - The boxer hit his adversary with great strength. Der. (n.) adversity; (adj.) adversarial.

adverse - (adj.) negative or in opposition to the interests of. e.g. - Adverse weather conditions made travel out of the question. Der. (n.) adversity; (adv.) adversely.

advocate - (n.) defender or supporter of a specific cause or issue; (syn.) proponent. e.g. - He is an advocate of that political party since he supports their policies. Der. (v.) advocate.

affable - (adj.) pleasant; friendly; (syn.) winsome, amiable, cordial. e.g. - James is an affable fellow and is pleasant company. Der. (n.) affability; (adv.) affably.

affiliation - (n.) an association or close relationship of members of a group; (syn.) alliance. e.g. - Many large American companies are actually an affiliation of several smaller companies. Der. (v.) affiliate.

affirm - (v.) to promise or declare positively. e.g. - I affirm that I will provide my assistance in the matter. You can depend on me. Der. (n.) affirmation.

afflict (with) - (v.) to cause pain or suffering. e.g. - She has been afflicted with cancer and is currently undergoing therapy. Der. (n.) affliction.

affluent - (adj.) rich; wealthy; well-to-do; well-off. e.g. - Alan is from an affluent family. They own five cars, three houses, and a yacht. Der. (n.) affluence; (adv.) affluently.

agrarian - (adj.) relating to farming or agriculture. e.g. - Agrarian businesses include the production of crops, as well as raising animals for resale.

ailment - (n.) an illness or disease. e.g. - He is suffering from a strange ailment and has been in bed for three weeks. Der. (v.) ail; (adj.) ailing.

alacrity - (n.) the willingness or readiness to carry out a specific action. e.g. - Sarah is an eager student and studies with alacrity.

alibi - (n.) an excuse used to free oneself from blame. e.g. - The suspect's alibi for the crime was that he was out of town when the murder took place.

alignment - (n.) the process of balancing or putting into line. e.g. - The desks in the classroom were in perfect alignment, with one exactly in front of the other. Der. (v.) align.

alliance - (n.) co-operation of allies or members; (syn.) affiliation. e.g. - The United Kingdom and the United States often form alliances, especially during times of war. Der. (adj.) allied.

allocate - (v.) to set aside in shares. e.g. - The profit was evenly allocated among all the partners of the company. Der. (n.) allocation; (adj.) allocated.

allot - (v.) to allocate or distribute in shares. e.g. - The father had a dozen cookies and allotted four of them to each of his three children. Der. (n.) allotment; (adj.) allotted.

allude (to) - (v.) to imply by inference or indirect speech. e.g. - He alluded to the idea that I had become fat by asking if I was wearing a larger dress size now. Der. (n.) allusion.

aloof - (adj.) arrogant; conceited. (syn.) stuck-up. e.g. - Bryce is so aloof that he often avoids our company. He feels that we aren't good enough for him. Der. (n.) aloofness; (adv.) aloofly.

altruistic - (adj.) relating to concern for the well-being of others. e.g. - He is one of the most altruistic men in the city as he constantly gives money to the poor. Der. (n.) altruism.

ambiance - (n.) atmosphere; surroundings. e.g. - The ambiance at the party was very cheerful. Everyone was in a great mood.

ambiguous - (adj.) unclear in meaning. e.g. - The professor's instructions were so ambiguous that none of the students could understand them. Der. (n.) ambiguity; (adv.) ambiguously.

ambush - (v.) to attack unexpectedly after lying in wait, esp. in battle. e.g. - The army was ambushed by their enemies, who had been hiding in a nearby forest. Der. (n.) ambush.

amiable - (adj.) pleasant; friendly; (syn.) affable, winsome, cordial. e.g. - Pam has an amiable personality and makes friends easily. Der. (adv.) amiably.

amiss - (adv.) wrong; mistaken. e.g. - I hope you won't take it amiss if I ask whether you have gained weight.

ancestor - (n.) a person born in a previous generation. e.g. - My ancestors left Europe to come to America 150 years ago.

animosity - (n.) feelings of hostility which can result in aggression. e.g. - Bob felt great animosity towards his boss for being unfairly fired.

antecedent - (adj.) relating to a preceding or previous event or circumstance. e.g. - A series of negotiations were antecedent to reaching a final agreement. Der. (n.) antecedent.

appalling - (adj.) causing shock or disbelief; (syn.) atrocious. e.g. - John's performance on the exam was appalling. Der. (v.) appall.

apparel - (n.) clothing; garments. e.g. - The department store sells all kinds of clothing, including men's, women's, and children's apparel.

apparent - (adj.) not hidden; open to sight; obvious; (syn.) evident. e.g. - It is apparent from your red nose that you have a cold. Der. (adv.) apparently.

appease - (v.) to calm or subdue. e.g. - We bought the whining children ice cream in an attempt to appease them. Der. (n.) appeasement; (adj.) appeasing.

appellation - (n.) a name or title. e.g. - Her appellation was the Queen of Sheba.

appliance - (n.) a piece of machinery or equipment used for a specific purpose, usually in the home or office. e.g. - The washing machine is such a useful appliance.

apply oneself – (id.) to work very hard on a specific task. e.g. - If we apply ourselves, we should be able to clean up the house in two hours.

apposite - (adj.) appropriate or suitable under the circumstances. e.g. - Louise is in the hospital, so I think that sending her some flowers would apposite. Der. (adv.) appositely.

apprehend - (v.) to capture a criminal who has escaped from the law. e.g. - The prisoner escaped while being transported, but was apprehended three days later. Der. (n.) apprehension; (adj.) apprehensible.

apprehension - (n.) fear caused by uncertainty. e.g.- Sally has a lot of apprehension about starting her new job. She's a nervous wreck. Der. (v.) apprehend; (adj.) apprehensive.

arduous - (adj.) exceptionally difficult or demanding. e.g. - The expedition to the North Pole was arduous and left the explorers exhausted. Der. (adv.) arduously.

as hard as nails – (id.) relating to a person who is strong and determined. e.g. - He won't give up. He's as hard as nails.

avid - (adj.) eager; enthusiastic. e.g. - He is an avid reader and reads three books a week. Der. (n.) avidity, avidness; (adv.) avidly.

Exercises – A

Instructions: Complete the sentences below, using one of the words beginning with the letter "A" from the previous section. Note that some gaps require a single word, while others may need a phrasal verb or idiomatic expression. You may also need to change the form of the word. The answers are provided at the end of book.

1) The _____ of the hospital with the health insurance company was an astute business venture.

2) He will _____ me to the movie, so I won't have to go alone.

3) There was a great deal of _____ between the two families because of a long-standing dispute.

4) The final exam is going to be _____, so you had better be well prepared.

5) That road will not be _____ because of the recent snowstorm.

6) This _____ can be used stick pieces of wood together.

7) The two teams were _____, and there was a great deal of rivalry between them.

8) The suspect had an _____ for the bank robbery since he was out of town at the time of the crime.

9) She _____ that I may have been lying by saying that my story was difficult to believe.

10) The _____ at the restaurant was so romantic with its candlelight and music.

Words – B

Instructions: Study the words below, paying attention to their meanings as well as how they are used in the example sentences. Then complete the exercise that follows.

babble - (v.) to talk quickly or incoherently. e.g. - Roseanne was babbling so fast about the accident that no one could understand her. Der. (n.) babble.

backing - (n.) the open expression of approval or support; endorsement. e.g. - She received the enthusiastic backing of her parents when she announced that she would marry the millionaire. Der. (v.) back.

baffle - (v.) to confuse or stupefy. e.g. - I can't understand this math homework. It completely baffles me.

banish - (v.) to drive out or force to leave. e.g. - You are banished from this club forever. Don't even try to come back here again. Der. (n.) banishment.

banner - (n.) a large piece of cloth bearing a message or national symbol; (syn.) ensign. e.g. - The fans displayed a message on a banner encouraging their team.

bargain - (n.) a sale or purchase at an advantageous price. e.g. - The motorcycle was a bargain. The original price was $1,000, and he paid only $200. Der. (v.) bargain.

barge - (n.) a long, flat-bottomed boat used to transport grains. e.g. - Many barges filled with grain travel down the Mississippi River.

barge in - (ph. v.) to enter unannounced. She always barges in without knocking.

barrier - (n.) something that inhibits or prevents progress or movement; (syn.) stumbling block, hindrance, obstacle. e.g. - A barrier was placed at the end of the street to prevent cars from entering.

bashful - (adj.) shy or self-conscious. e.g. - Mary is so bashful that she often finds it difficult to make new friends. Der. (v.) abash.

battle - (n.) a fight between two opposing armies; (syn.) combat. e.g. - Many soldiers died from gunshot wounds inflicted in the battle. Der. (v.) battle.

be a wreck - (id.) to be in very bad physical condition, esp. from nervousness or exhaustion. e.g. - Mary is a wreck about her upcoming hospital stay.

be caught red-handed - (id.) to be discovered during the commission of criminal activities. e.g. - He was caught red-handed as he attempted to put the stolen merchandise in his pocket.

be in ruins - (id.) to be totally destroyed. e.g. - The town was in ruins after the hurricane.

be of strong moral fiber - (id.) to be of good moral character. e.g. - Dylan would never lie or steal. He is of strong moral fiber.

beating around the bush - (id.) to avoid talking about a certain topic. e.g. - I tried to get an answer out of her, but she kept on beating around the bush.

beckon - (v.) to call forward. e.g. - The teacher is beckoning you to come forward to the board.

belittle - (v.) to cause to feel inferior. e.g. - Sam always belittles his wife by telling her how stupid she is. Actually, she is quite intelligent.

bequest - (n.) the action of leaving money or specific property to another person upon an individual's death. e.g. - A bequest in my uncle's will specifically states that I shall receive $10,000 when he dies. Der. (v.) bequeath.

beseech - (v.) to beg; (syn.) implore; entreat; (p. part.) besought. e.g. - The victim besought the attacker not to kill him.

beset - (v.) to cause trouble or difficulties. e.g. - Tina has been beset with difficulties all her life.

beside yourself – (id.) to be very nervous or upset. e.g. - I am just beside myself waiting for the results of my test.

beverage - (n.) any alcoholic or non-alcoholic drink. e.g. - I was thirsty and wanted to drink a cold beverage.

beyond my wildest dreams - (id.) to be better than your highest expectations. e.g. - My vacation in Rome was beyond my wildest dreams.

biased - (adj.) relating to prejudice caused by an unfair or irrational belief or preference. e.g. - A judge must never be biased, but must treat all people fairly and equally. Der. (n.) bias; (v.) bias.

bigoted - (adj.) relating to prejudice because of race, color, or national origin. e.g. - He is so bigoted. He always says negative and inappropriate things about people of other races. Der. (n.) bigot.

bill - (n.) a piece of paper money used in the United States. e.g. - The pockets of his jeans were full of dollar bills and various coins.

bland - (adj.) tasteless or lacking in flavor; (syn.) insipid. e.g. - These potatoes are bland. I think they could use some salt. Der. (n.) blandness; (adv.) blandly.

blandishment - (n.) compliment. e.g. - Mike gave me a nice blandishment yesterday. He told me that I was the most beautiful girl he'd ever seen. Der. (v.) blandish.

bleak - (adj.) hopeless; depressing. e.g. - What bleak weather! Gray sky and rain get me down. Der. (n.) bleakness; (adv.) bleakly.

blister - (n.) a raised area of skin which contains water or fluid. e.g. - These shoes are too small. They have given me blisters on my feet.

blow - (n.) the action of striking or hitting. e.g. - The boxer fell to the floor when struck by his opponent's blow.

blow your chances - (id.) to lose all opportunities for success in an activity. e.g. - He blew his chances of buying a car by losing all his money gambling.

blue - (id.) relating to extreme sadness or depression. e.g. - Julie felt blue after her boyfriend left her. I've never seen her so down.

bluff - (n.) the steep side of a mountain; cliff. e.g. - An excellent view of the city can be seen when looking down from the nearby bluff.

blunder - (n.) error; mistake. e.g. - The accident resulted from his blunder in failing to signal his turn.

blunt - (adj.) not sharp; dull. e.g. - The victim was struck with a blunt object, such as a flat rock or brick. Der. (adv.) bluntly.

blurry - (adj.) unclear or lacking in focus. e.g. - My vision is always blurry when I'm not wearing my glasses. Der. (n.) blur, blurriness; (v.) blur; (adj.) blurred; (adv.) blurrily.

blurt - (v.) to say something suddenly and unexpectedly. e.g. - He blurted out the location of the surprise party.

bogus - (adj.) not authentic; fake; (syn.) phony. e.g. - The bogus painting of the "Mona Lisa" is often mistaken for the genuine one.

bolster - (v.) to raise or increase by supporting the cause or interest of something. e.g. - Going to Disneyland bolstered the spirits of the terminally-ill children.

boom - (v.) to experience great success or expansion; prosper. e.g. - The college is building new classrooms because enrollment is booming. Der. (n.) boom.

booth - (n.) an area enclosed by temporary walls on three or more sides. e.g. - He placed a telephone call from a public phone booth.

bored to tears - (id.) very bored. e.g. - The lesson was hardly interesting. In fact, I was bored to tears.

bountiful - (adj.) existing in great quantity or variety. e.g. - That supermarket has a bountiful selection of different types of food. Der. (n.) bounty; (adv.) bountifully.

box office - (id.) the cashier's office at a movie theater. e.g. - We bought our tickets at the movie theater box office.

brawl - (v.) to fight or engage in physical contact. e.g. - Three young men were brawling in the street. As a result, two were sent to the hospital. Der. (n.) brawl.

breach - (v.) to break or violate the law. e.g. - If you park in a prohibited area, you will breach the law. Der. (n.) breach.

break down - (ph. v.) to destroy or remove. e.g. - Their relationship broke down due to their constant arguments about money.

breed - (n.) class, kind, or type. e.g. - The zoo displayed numerous breeds of animals. Der. (v.) breed.

bribe - (n.) money given to influence the judgment of a public official. e.g. - He offered money to the policeman as a bribe in order to avoid paying a heavy fine. Der. (v.) bribe.

brim - (n.) the top edge of a cup. e.g. - That cup is filled to the brim. If you bump it, it will spill.

broil - (v.) to cook by placing under fire or heat. e.g. - He broiled steaks and pork chops under the gas fire in the oven. Der. (adj.) broiled.

buck - (id.) dollar. e.g. - I bought this sweater for twelve bucks.

budge - (v.) to move sthg with difficulty. e.g. - Alan tried to move the heavy cabinet, but it wouldn't budge.

bug - (v.) to place small listening devices secretly in hidden places. e.g. - The police bugged the hiding place of the Mafia in an attempt to listen to their secret conversations. Der. (n.) bug.

bump - (n.) a small, raised area. e.g. - Janice had a bump on her head from hitting it on the steering wheel of the car in the accident. Der. (v.) bump.

buoy - (n.) a floating object that indicates a dangerous area in a waterway. e.g. - Don't swim beyond the red and white buoys floating in the water. It's too deep to swim out there. Der. (n.) buoyancy; (adj.) buoyant; (adv.) buoyantly.

bureaucratic - (adj.) relating to the administration of the government. e.g. - I had a lot of bureaucratic hassle at the court house this morning when I went to re-new my driver's license. Der. (n.) bureaucracy.

burial - (n.) the action of placing something under the ground, esp. the body of the deceased in a funeral. e.g. - The dog has many bad habits, the most annoying of which is the burial of bones in our front yard. Der. (v.) bury.

bustle - (v.) to move hurriedly, esp. in order to prepare something. e.g. - Anne had to bustle around this morning. She overslept and was late for work.

butter sbdy up - (id.) to win someone's favor through flattery. e.g. - He tried to butter me up by saying how beautiful I looked today.

by leaps and bounds - (id.) with incredible or amazing speed. e.g. - The world population crisis is evident in countries such as India, where the population has grown by leaps and bounds.

Exercises – B

Instructions: Complete the sentences below, using one of the words beginning with the letter "B" from the previous section. Note that some gaps require a single word, while others may need a phrasal verb or idiomatic expression. You may also need to change the form of the word. The answers are provided at the end of book.

1) He wouldn't give be a straight answer, but just kept on _____.

2) She had dollar _____ and coins with her in her purse.

3) You will _____ your rental agreement if you leave without paying twelve months' rent.

4) The ship entered the prohibited zone, even though there were _____ demarcating the area.

5) Their business relationship _____ because they couldn't agree on a management strategy.

6) Her food is always so _____ since she refuses to use any spice or seasoning.

7) She _____ her husband with constant insults. I don't know how he puts up with it.

8) The last section of the exam _____ me. I doubt if I got a single question correct.

9) Telling me I was beautiful and intelligent was such a nice _____.

10) I was _____ in class today. There was nothing new or interesting in the class material.

Words – C

Instructions: Study the words below, paying attention to their meanings as well as how they are used in the example sentences. Then complete the exercise that follows.

cagey - (adj.) relating to the use of cleverness and dishonesty. e.g. - The cagey criminal robbed me after visiting my home under the pretense of being an insurance salesman.

calamity - (n.) disaster; catastrophe. e.g. - The San Francisco earthquake was one of America's worst natural calamities.

call for sthg - (id.) to make something necessary or required. e.g. - This recipe calls for white wine.

calling - (n.) vocation. e.g. - He felt that his calling was to be a doctor.

campaign - (n.) participation as a candidate in a political election. e.g. - He was an assistant in the U.S. Presidential campaign. Der. (v.) campaign.

candor - (n.) honesty; frankness. e.g. - If I can speak with candor, I must tell you that your behavior is entirely unacceptable. Der. (adj.) candid; (adv.) candidly.

capitulate - (v.) to give up or surrender in battle. e.g. - The army capitulated after the enemy's heavy attack. Der. (n.) capitulation.

capsize - (v.) to overturn a boat in a waterway. e.g. - The passenger fell overboard into the water when the boat capsized.

carcass - (n.) the body of a dead animal. e.g. - The carcass of a dead dog, which had been hit by a car, was lying in the center of the road.

carnivorous - (adj.) relating to animals that consume meat. e.g. - Animals such as dogs are carnivorous. They do not eat grass, but rather eat meat. Der (n.) carnivore.

cask - (n.) a round wooden container used for storing alcoholic beverages; barrel. e.g. - Whiskey and beer are usually stored in large casks when they are manufactured.

cast aspersions on sbdy's character - (id.) to damage someone's reputation through rumors or gossip. e.g. - I would never cast aspersions on his character. In fact, I know that he is a very nice person.

catch - (v.)(met.) to hear or to understand. e.g. - Did you catch what he just said?

cavity - (n.) a small hole in something. e.g. - If you eat too much candy, you will get cavities in your teeth.

censure - (v.) to experience public criticism by one's colleagues. e.g. - The lawyer was censured by the state legal committee for attempting to steal money from a client. Der. (n.) censure.

champion - (v.) to support a cause or campaign strongly. e.g. - He championed the abolition of the death penalty.

chant - (v.) to sing in a monotonous voice, esp. during religious worship. e.g. - It is difficult for Debbie to sing with a group since she chants in a monotone and finds it difficult to sing a melody

chaperon - (n.) an individual who accompanies or goes with another. e.g. - An attractive young man was her chaperon for the evening. Der. (v.) chaperon.

charge (with) - (v.) to accuse an individual of the commission of a crime. e.g. - The police came to the suspect's house with legal documents to charge her with the crime of robbery.

charming - (adj.) exceptionally pleasant, as if magical. e.g. - David is a charming man. He has many friends since it is so easy to enjoy his company. Der. (n.) charm; (v.) charm.

chaste - (adj.) pure or clean in character, esp. sexually. e.g. - A rapist can hardly be considered chaste. Der. (n.) chastity.

cheat on - (id.) to be unfaithful to one's spouse or romantic partner. e.g. - Tom is filing for divorce because his wife was cheating on him.

check sthg out - (id.) to look at or verify something. e.g. - Check out the story in this newspaper. It's really amazing.

checkered past - (id.) to have undesirable experiences in one's past. e.g. - Bob doesn't speak about his life in Chicago. He must have a checkered past.

chew - (v.) to move the teeth together and apart when eating. e.g. - Food must be chewed well before swallowing.

chortle - (v.) to laugh. e.g. - The funny joke made us all chortle.

cinder - (n.) a small gray fragment which remains after a fire is extinguished. e.g. - Small cinders drifted in the smoke from the factory chimney.

civilian - (n.) an individual not on duty in the armed services. e.g. - Since the soldier was not on active duty in the army, he was dressed as a civilian.

clandestine - (adj.) being done or carried out in secrecy. e.g. - The clandestine government operation was known only to a select group of politicians. Der. (adv.) clandestinely.

clarify - (v.) to make clear in meaning. e.g. - The teacher explained the homework again in order to clarify the instructions. Der. (n.) clarity, clarification.

classify - (v.) to place into groups or categories. e.g. - The advertisements were classified according to employment opportunities and items offered for sale. Der. (n.) classification; (adj.) classified.

clip - (v.) to cut quickly, esp. with a scissors. He showed me an article that he had clipped out of a magazine.

clot - (n.) the formation of blood into a hardened lump. e.g. - It looks as though that wound will stop bleeding now. I think a clot is beginning to form. Der. (v.) clot; (adj.) clotted.

clutter - (n.) a disorganized collection of various items. e.g. - It took Laura two days to organize the clutter left on her desk while she was away from the office on vacation. Der. (adj.) cluttered.

coax - (v.) to influence, persuade, or manipulate; (syn.) cajole. e.g. - Christine was not in the mood to go to the party, but we coaxed her into going by saying that her boyfriend would be there.

cog - (n.) a small tooth-like piece on a wheel-shaped gear. e.g. - The clock was not working because a small cog on the inside had broken off.

cogent - (adj.) logical and credible. e.g. - Saying that the earth is flat is hardly a cogent statement. Der. (adv.) cogently.

collaboration - (n.) the action of working together with others; (syn.) cooperation. e.g. - The collaboration of all the factory workers made everyone's job easier. Der. (v.) collaborate.

colossal - (adj.) amazing or incredible in size. e.g. - The elephant is a colossal animal, often weighing several tons.

comb - (v.)(met.) to search extensively for something, esp. with difficulty. e.g. - The police are combing the city in search of the escaped criminal.

commemorate - (v.) to serve as a reminder for events of particular historical significance. e.g. - Veteran's Day is celebrated to commemorate the lives lost in former wars. Der. (n.) commemoration; (adj.) commemorative.

commence - (v.) to begin; to start. e.g. - The T.V. program commenced at 8:00 and finished at 9:00. Der. (n.) commencement.

commended - (adj.) deserving of special praise, notice, or attention. e.g. - The soldier was commended for bravery in battle by receiving a Purple Heart Medal. Der. (n.) commendation; (v.) commend.

commentary - (n.) a systematic explanation of events. e.g. - He is a sports announcer and often provides commentary during televised football games. Der. (n.) commentator; (v.) comment.

commercial - (adj.) relating to business or finance. Banking and investments are commercial activities. Der. (n.) commerce; (adv.) commercially.

commodity - (n.) any item that can be bought and sold in the marketplace. e.g. - Gold and silver are precious commodities that are readily exchanged in the marketplace.

compassion - (n.) the state of being full of mercy. e.g. - The doctor displayed great compassion toward the dying man. Der. (adj.) compassionate; (adv.) compassionately.

compel - (v.) to cause or bring out through force or pressure. e.g. - His parents compelled him to attend college, although he didn't want to. Der. (n.) compulsion; (adj.) compelling.

component - (n.) an integral or necessary part of something. e.g. - All of the components must be working in order for the machine to function properly.

comprehensive - (adj.) complete; all-inclusive. e.g. - The examination is comprehensive. It covers the entire textbook. Der. (n.) comprehensiveness; (adv.) comprehensively.

compress - (v.) to apply with great pressure. e.g. - This machine can compress a large amount of garbage into one small package. Der. (n.) compress; (adj.) compressed.

compulsory - (adj.) required; necessary; obligatory; (syn.) mandatory. e.g. - Class attendance is compulsory. You are required to attend.

concatenation - (n.) the series of items linked in different orders. e.g. - There are many concatenations of human DNA. Der. (v.) concatenate.

concentrate - (n.) a product that has been reduced in size as a result of dehydration. e.g. - This new dish-washing liquid is a concentrate. Only one-quarter of the normal amount should be used. Der. (n.) concentration; (v.) concentrate; (adj.) concentrated.

concoction - (n.) a food or drink that has been prepared from a combination of ingredients which are often mysterious or unknown. e.g. - Marisa refused to tell us the ingredients of the concoction she had made, saying that the recipe was a secret. Der. (v.) concoct; (adj.) concocted.

condone - (v.) to view as unimportant; to overlook. Your behavior is unacceptable, and I cannot condone it. Der. (adj.) condonable.

conducive (to) - (adj.) beneficial; helpful. e.g. - A quiet weekend in the countryside is conducive to relaxation. Der. (v.) conduce.

confection - (n.) any sweet or dessert; food made with sugar. e.g. - That store sells all kinds of confections, including chocolate, cakes, and cookies. Der. (adj.) confectionary.

confession - (n.) the admission of guilt or wrongdoing. e.g. - After several denials, the suspect finally signed a full confession of the crime. Der. (v.) confess.

confidential - (adj.) secret; private; personal. e.g. - This letter is confidential and should be read only by the person to whom it is addressed. Der. (n.) confidence; (v.) confide; (adv.) confidentially.

confine - (v.) to cause to become limited in room or space. e.g. - The prisoner was confined to his cell twenty-three hours a day and often dreamed of freedom. Der. (n.) confinement; (adj.) confined.

conflagration - (n.) a great fire. e.g. - The fire department was called to put out the conflagration.

conform (to) - (v.) to agree to or comply with a standard. e.g. - Those individuals who do not conform to the rules of the club will be denied membership. Der. (n.) conformity.

congregation - (n.) a gathering of individuals. e.g. - There was a large congregation of people at the war memorial service. Der. (v.) congregate.

conjugation - (n.) the formation of pairs or groups. e.g. - Many grammatical exercises involve the conjugation of verbs. Der. (v.) conjugate.

consensus - (n.) agreement by members of a group. e.g. - After fifteen minutes of discussion, the group finally reached a consensus about what restaurant to go to.

consistency - (1)(n.) texture; firmness; (2)(n.) the quality of not changing. e.g. - (1) The consistency of the apple was too soft. We knew that it was not fit to eat. (2) Brandy has shown consistency in her performance at college this year. She has received A's all semester. Der. (adj.) consistent; (adv.) consistently.

console - (v.) to soothe or comfort. e.g. - Terri was crying, so we tried to console her by saying that everything was going to be alright. Der. (n.) consolation.

consolidate - (v.) to join together; unite; merge. e.g. - The two companies consolidated to form a new, larger company. Der. (n.) consolidation; (adj.) consolidated.

conspicuous - (adj.) noticeable; capable of drawing attention. e.g. - Tim's wealth was conspicuous by the large amounts of money he spent. Der. (n.) conspicuousness; (adv.) conspicuously.

constituent - (n.) a citizen of a particular political district who is eligible to vote in elections. e.g. - The constituents of Dallas will vote for a new mayor in the upcoming elections. Der. (n.) constituency.

consumer - (n.) an individual who buys goods in the marketplace. e.g. - Increased purchasing by consumers has resulted in an improvement in the economy. Der. (v.) consume; (n.) consumption.

consummate - (v.) to bring to a conclusion. e.g. - The agreement was consummated when the contract was signed. Der. (n.) consummation; (adj.) consummated.

contagious - (adj.) infectious; transmitted from one individual to another. e.g. - Many childhood diseases are contagious. If one child becomes ill, other children living in the same house will also become ill. Der. (n.) contagion.

contaminate - (v.) to cause to become infected, polluted, or poisoned. e.g. - Many American rivers used to be contaminated by pollution from nearby factories. Der. (n.) contamination.

contemplate - (v.) to think about or consider. e.g. - The great philosophers often contemplated the meaning of life. Der. (n.) contemplation; (adj.) contemplative; (adv.) contemplatively.

contemporary - (adj.) modern; current. e.g. - She hates old-fashioned things so her house is filled only with contemporary furniture. Der. (adv.) contemporarily.

contempt - (n.) hatred or disgust; (syn.) enmity. e.g. - Great contempt was shown towards the criminal by the judge, who said that the crimes shocked society. Der. (adj.) contemptible, contemptuous.

contend (with) - (v.) to deal with; to manage a difficult situation. e.g. - Police officers have to contend with danger and violence in their jobs. Der. (n.) contention.

contiguous - (adj.) adjoining; neighboring; sharing a common boundary. e.g. - The northern border of the United States is contiguous with Canada. Der. (n.) contiguity; (adv.) contiguously.

contingent - (adj.) dependent upon unpredictable causes or events. e.g. - Our trip to the beach tomorrow is contingent upon the weather. Der. (n.) contingency; (adv.) contingently.

contravene - (v.) to oppose or act against the desires or wishes of another individual. e.g. - Children who contravene the wishes of their parents often receive punishment. Der. (n.) contravention.

contrition - (n.) the feeling of deep sorrow or regret about one's wrongdoings; (syn.) remorse, penitence. e.g. - The criminal felt great contrition for his crimes and was filled with regret. Der. (adj.) contrite.

contrive - (v.) to devise or plan, esp. in artistic form. e.g. - After months of planning, the prisoners finally contrived a way to escape. Der. (adj.) contrived.

controversial - (adj.) relating to discussion in or disagreement among the public with respect to a specific topic. e.g. - Capital punishment and abortion are highly controversial topics.

convalesce - (v.) to recover health after an extended illness or operation; (syn.) recuperate. e.g. - Samantha is at home convalescing after having surgery on her back. Der. (n.) convalescence; (adj.) convalescent.

convict (of) - (v.) to send a criminal to prison for his crime. e.g. - Michael is serving life in prison as a result of being convicted of murder. Der. (n.) convict, conviction; (adj.) convicted.

convivial - (adj.) cheerful; friendly. e.g. - He has a convivial personality and is very outgoing. Der. (n.) conviviality; (adv.) convivially.

cooperation - (n.) the action of working together with others; (syn.) collaboration. e.g. - The cooperation of three cardiology specialists was needed to diagnose the patient's heart condition. Der. (v.) cooperate; (adj.) cooperative; (adv.) cooperatively.

coordinate - (v.) to act or work together. e.g. - The work of several departments of the company was coordinated in order to make operations more efficient. Der. (n.) coordinator; (n.) coordination; (adj.) coordinated.

cordial - (adj.) friendly; (syn.) affable, amiable, winsome. e.g. - She is quite cordial and makes friends easily. Der. (adv.) cordially.

core - (adj.) relating to the basic or central part. e.g. The core courses must be taken during a student's first year at this college. After that, the students may choose from more specialized courses.

cork - (n.) a porous substance that is commonly used to seal the tops of bottles of wine. e.g. - A special opener is needed to remove the cork from the top of a wine bottle.

count me in - (id.) to want to participate in an activity. e.g. - I'll come to the party with you. Count me in.

counterfeit - (n.) false copies of paper money. e.g. - This money is counterfeit. It is not authentic and is, therefore, worthless. Der. (v.) counterfeit; (adj.) counterfeit.

coup - (n.) a revolutionary group that seeks to overthrow an existing government, esp. with the use of violence. e.g. - The Parliament building was seized during the coup as the rebels attempted to take control of the government.

covert - (adj.) hidden or secretive. e.g. - The details of the covert military operation were known only to the president and a few of his close assistants. Der. (n.) covertness; (adv.) covertly; (ant.) overt.

cover-up - (n.) the action of hiding despicable or blameworthy actions or events. e.g. - The cover-up of the crime involved the destruction of key evidence. Der. (ph. v.) cover up.

coy - (adj.) flirtatious or coquettish. e.g. - The woman was very coy in gaining the affection of the man. Der. (adv.) coyly.

crack sbdy up - (id.) to amuse someone. e.g. - Juan's funny jokes really crack me up.

crate - (n.) a wooden box-like container. e.g. - The oranges were transported to the grocery store in a wooden crate.

creep - (n.) an obnoxious or unpleasant person. e.g. - Don't go out with him. He's really a creep.

crevice - (n.) a narrow crack. e.g. - Barbara fell down when her heel got caught in a crevice in the sidewalk.

crimson - (adj.) dark red. e.g. - Blood is crimson in color.

crushed - (id.) to be very disappointed. e.g. - She was crushed when her boyfriend left her.

culminate (in) - (v.) to bring to a conclusion. e.g. - The graduation ceremony culminates in the distribution of diplomas to the class. Der. (n.) culmination.

cultivation - (n.) the process of preparing the land for planting. e.g. - Cultivation begins in the spring when the top soil is turned over in order to prepare the ground for seeds or plants. Der. (v.) cultivate; (adj.) cultivated.

cumbersome - (adj.) troublesome; difficult; heavy. e.g. - Jennifer's journey was cumbersome since she carried two huge suitcases with her. Der. (v.) encumber.

cumulative - (adj.) the total sum of separate parts. e.g. - The cumulative sum of 20 and 20 is 40. Der. (v.) cumulate; (adv.) cumulatively.

cunning - (adj.) relating to the use of dishonesty and manipulation to achieve one's ambitions; sly; (syn.) sneaky. e.g. - Jeff doesn't really love Debra. He's just being cunning in order to get what he wants from her. Der. (n.) cunning; (adv.) cunningly.

custody - (n.) control or guardianship over a person by an individual in authority. e.g. - Anne was granted custody of the children in the divorce. They now live with her. Der. (adj.) custodial.

cut off your nose to spite your face - (id.) to hurt oneself by seeking revenge on others. e.g. - I know that you don't like your teacher, but telling her that she's stupid was cutting off your nose to spite your face.

Exercises – C

Instructions: Complete the sentences below, using one of the words beginning with the letter "C" from the previous section. Note that some gaps require a single word, while others may need a phrasal verb or idiomatic expression. You may also need to change the form of the word. The answers are provided at the end of book.

1) We _____ when he told the funny joke.

2) The boat _____, and the passengers fell into the sea

3) There was a secret _____ in the wall where he had hidden a gun.

4) I had so much _____ in the house that my roommate told me to get organized.

5) They had a _____ relationship and had to meet in secret places.

6) The _____ of the members of staff will ensure that the project is completed more quickly.

7) The college _____ its English courses into three categories: beginner, intermediate, and advanced.

8) After weeks of refusing my request, my boss finally _____ and said I could take my vacation when I wanted.

9) That little English town is so _____ with its cottages and cobblestone streets.

10) She couldn't put forward a _____ argument for her point of view, so we weren't convinced that her idea was a good one.

Words – D

Instructions: Study the words below, paying attention to their meanings as well as how they are used in the example sentences. Then complete the exercise that follows.

damp - (adj.) slightly wet or moist. e.g. - His forehead was damp because he had been sweating. He wiped it dry with a handkerchief. Der. (n.) damp; (v.) dampen.

dapper - (adj.) very well dressed. e.g. - He looked dapper in his new suit.

dash - (n.) a small portion of something added to something else. e.g. - A dash of salt should be added to the food.

debris - (n.) the remaining broken pieces of something. e.g. - There was a lot of debris on the road after the accident, including fragments of broken glass and pieces of metal.

deceased - (adj.) relating to a person who has died. e.g. - My father is deceased. He died ten years ago. Der. (n.) decedent.

deciduous - (adj.) relating to trees which lose their leaves seasonally. e.g. - Deciduous trees in Vermont turn to beautiful shades of red, orange, and yellow before losing their leaves every fall.

decorous - (adj.) correct in behavior; in good taste. e.g. - The fireman behaved in a most decorous way during the blaze and cannot be blamed for the deaths that occurred. Der. (n.) decorum; (adv.) decorously.

defect - (n.) a lack of proper function which prevents use of a machine. e.g. - The stereo had a defect in its sound system and would not play the CD properly. Der. (adj.) defective; (adv.) defectively.

defile - (v.) to cause to become unclean or unchaste. e.g. - The environment is being defiled with all types of pollution and litter. Der. (n.) defilement; (adj.) defiled.

deft - (adj.) possessing great skill or ability. e.g. - Paula is quite deft at knitting. She made this sweater in only twelve hours. Der. (adv.) deftly.

defunct - (adj.) no longer existing or operating; no longer active. e.g. - Due to a lack of interest by its members, the club is now defunct.

defy - (v.) to accomplish something that is considered impossible or improper. e.g. - He defied his parents by getting married when he was only sixteen, although they had forbidden it. Der. (n.) defiance; (adj.) defiant; (adv.) defiantly.

deliberation - (n.) careful consideration of a topic, including reasons for and against. e.g. - After careful deliberation of all the advantages and disadvantages, she finally decided to attend college. Der. (v.) deliberate; (adj.) deliberate.

deluge - (n.) a sudden downpour of rain or water. e.g. - A sudden deluge of rain caused flooding in the city. Der. (v.) deluge.

demeanor - (n.) behavior, manner, or temperament. e.g. - This job requires a person with a pleasant demeanor because you will constantly be working with the public.

demented - (adj.) crazy; insane. e.g. - Why are you acting so demented? Have you gone crazy or something? Der. (n.) dementedness; (adv.) dementedly.

demise - (n.) destruction or downfall. e.g. - Excessive gambling led to his demise. He lost all of his possessions as a result of his uncontrollable habit.

demoralize - (v.) to discourage; to weaken the spirit of. e.g. - Carmen was demoralized when she failed her driving test the fourth time.

denial - (n.) statement that an accusation is false. e.g. - The President issued a full denial of any involvement in the break-in, saying that any rumors were untrue. Der. (v.) deny.

denomination - (n.) size of a value of paper money. e.g. - The bank robbers stole $10,000 in $100 and $50 denominations. Der. (v.) denominate.

denounce - (v.) to show to be false, wrong, or evil. e.g. - He denounced smoking, saying that it was a disgusting and dangerous habit. Der. (n.) denouncement.

dense - (adj.) thick or heavy. e.g. - A dense snowfall caused the highway department to close all the roads. Der. (adv.) densely.

depict - (v.) to show in the form of a picture or photograph. This photograph depicts my mother when she was a child. Der. (n.) depiction.

deplore - (v.) to consider as deserving of contempt or disapproval. e.g. - The teacher deplored the students who hadn't done their homework and expressed her disapproval. Der. (adj.) deplorable; (adv.) deplorably.

deposit - (v.) to place money in a bank account. e.g. - I am trying to save money by depositing $200 into my bank account every month. Der. (n.) deposit.

deranged - (adj.) mentally disturbed; insane; crazy. e.g. - Deranged individuals, such as psychopaths or sociopaths, are in need of psychological treatment. Der. (v.) derange.

desolate - (adj.) filled with sorrow or despair as a result of loneliness; (syn.) forlorn. e.g. - Thomas felt <u>desolate</u> when he moved to Houston. Since he was new in town, he didn't have any friends and was often lonely. Der. (n.) desolation; (adj.) desolating.

despair - (v.) to feel hopelessness or extreme disappointment; (syn.) despondency. e.g. - The businessman <u>despaired</u> that he would never be successful when his second business failed. Der. (n.) despair.

desperation - (n.) hopelessness; despair. e.g. - The poor woman hadn't eaten in days and, in <u>desperation</u>, she stole food from the grocery store. Der. (adj.) desperate; (adv.) desperately.

despicable - (adj.) deserving of hate; (syn.) odious. e.g. - The crimes that he committed are <u>despicable</u>, and he has many enemies. Der. (adv.) despicably.

despondency - (n.) despair; depression. e.g. - In his <u>despondency</u>, he contemplated whether his life had meaning. Der. (adj.) despondent. Der. (adv.) despondently.

destine - (v.) to determine the outcome of something in advance, esp. by fate. e.g. - He is a very smart boy and is <u>destined</u> to have a bright future. Der. (n.) destiny; (adj.) destined.

detention - (n.) the process of delaying or holding back, esp. for questioning or punishment. e.g. - He was held in <u>detention</u> after school as punishment for failing to do his homework. Der. (v.) detain.

deterrent - (n.) the prevention or discouragement of illegal or improper behavior. e.g. - The death penalty is considered to be a <u>deterrent</u> to the commission of the crime of murder, although statistics show that the murder rate increases every year. Der. (v.) deter.

detract (from) - (v.) to make less in terms of value or importance. e.g. - The crack in the vase <u>detracted</u> from its value.

devoted - (adj.) strongly committed to a purpose or cause. e.g. - He is a <u>devoted</u> doctor and often works without pay. Der. (n.) devotion; (v.) devote.

devour - (v.) to eat or use up in great quantity. e.g. - The hungry dog <u>devoured</u> its food.

dig up - (id.) to discover as a result of searching extensively. e.g. - Joe searched through his closet, trying to <u>dig up</u> something to wear.

diligent - (adj.) relating to the exercise of caution and determination. e.g. - You must be <u>diligent</u> when driving on interstate highways in order to avoid accidents. Der. (n.) diligence; (adv.) diligently.

dilute - (v.) to add water to a mixture. e.g. - The orange juice concentrate should be diluted and mixed before serving.

dingy - (adj.) dirty; unclean. e.g. - The hotel was so dingy that it looked like it hadn't been cleaned in months.

disclose - (v.) to uncover or cause to become known. e.g. - The bank robber finally disclosed the location of the hidden money after undergoing extensive questioning. Der. (n.) disclosure.

disconcerted - (adj.) very discouraged; disillusioned. e.g. - My cousin was disconcerted when he realized that his new job wasn't what he wanted after all. Der. (v.) disconcert.

discontented - (adj.) unhappy; displeased. e.g. - Many students become discontented with college and decide to drop out. Der (n.) discontentment, discontent.

discrepancy - (n.) disagreement or inconsistency between or among various things. e.g. - There was a discrepancy between the two different versions of the story. Der. (adj.) discrepant; (adv.) discrepantly.

disjointed - (adj.) lacking in sequence, order, or organization. e.g. - The professor's explanation was totally disjointed. As a result, none of the students understood him. Der. (v.) disjoint.

dismal - (adj.) being of particularly bad quality; disastrous; (syn.) wretched. e.g. - The weather is so dismal today with all this sleet and rain. Der. (adv.) dismally.

dismantle - (v.) to take a machine apart into pieces; disassemble. e.g. - She dismantled her furniture before moving into her new house since the individual pieces of wood would be easier to carry.

disparity - (n.) disagreement; (syn.) incongruity. e.g. - There seems to be some disparity between the story he told and the facts.

dispatch - (v.) to send, esp. quickly. e.g. - The letter was dispatched to you by courier on Thursday. Der. (n.) dispatch.

dispense - (v.) to give out in shares or measured parts. e.g. - My parents always dispense advice without me asking for it.

disposition - (n.) mood or character. e.g. - His disposition was great today. I have never seen him so cheerful. Der. (v.) dispose.

dissension - (n.) disagreement; conflict; controversy. e.g. - There is some dissension about what happened. Everyone seems to have a different version of the events. Der. (v.) dissent.

dissolute - (adj.) indulgent. e.g. - If you have dissolute eating habits, you will become fat. Der. (n.) dissolution; (adv.) dissolutely.

divergence - (n.) separation; movement apart; disunion. e.g. - Their divergence in personal opinions causes many arguments. Der. (v.) diverge; (adj.) divergent.

diversification - (n.) the action of providing variety. e.g. - This college offers great diversification to its students, with programs ranging from animal science to hair styling. Der. (v.) diversify; (adj.) diversified.

diversion - (n.) a change of course in direction or activity. e.g. - There is a traffic diversion in the center of town because the road is being repaired. Der. (v.) divert; (adj.) diverted.

domain - (n.) territory. e.g. - Don't enter this room. It is my private domain.

domestic - (adj.) relating to or coming from a specific country. e.g. - Many domestic American wines are produced in California. Der. (n.) domesticity; (v.) domesticate; (adj.) domesticated.

domineering - (adj.) controlling or influencing excessively. e.g. - She is a domineering woman and is always telling her husband what to do. Der. (n.) domination; (v.) domineer; (adv.) domineeringly.

don't rain on my parade - (id.) don't discourage me. e.g. - I just know I'm going to win the lottery so don't rain on my parade!

downfall - (n.) a situation which results in a catastrophe. e.g. - His downfall came from gambling. In fact, he lost the family fortune.

dregs - (n.) a substance that remains after a liquid has been removed from a container. e.g. - He poured the beer into a glass, leaving only the dregs at the bottom of the bottle.

drench - (v.) to become full or covered with water or moisture; (syn.) soak. e.g. - Marco got drenched when he was caught in the rain without an umbrella. Der. (adj.) drenched.

drive - (n.) motivation or impulse. e.g. - John is one of the laziest people I know. He has absolutely no drive. Der. (v.) drive; (adj.) driven.

drive a hard bargain - (id.) to be difficult to negotiate with. e.g. - He's not going to change his mind. He drives a hard bargain.

drop a hint - (id.) to give someone subtle ideas about something in order to express one's likes or dislikes. e.g. - He dropped a hint that he would like a new tie for his birthday.

drop in - (id.) to visit someone's home without having arranged a specific time. e.g. - Drop in and see me sometime!

dubious - (adj.) doubtful in quality. e.g. - He told us a dubious story about a series of unbelievable events that he claimed had caused his delay. Der. (n.) dubiety, dubiousness; (adv.) dubiously.

duplication - (n.) the action of making copies of an object. e.g. - The teacher realized that the student had copied his homework from his friend since there was some duplication in the mistakes that were made. Der. (v.) duplicate; (adj.) duplicated.

duplicitous - (adj.) relating to living a deceptive or double life. e.g. - The duplicitous man had two wives, neither of whom knew of the other's existence. Der. (adv.) duplicitously.

dwindle - (v.) to decrease in size or amount. e.g. - The size of the class has dwindled. We began with twenty-five students and now have only five. Der. (adj.) dwindling.

dysfunction - (n.) failure to function properly. e.g. - The dysfunction in their relationship caused the couple to file for divorce. Der. (adj.) dysfunctional.

Exercises – D

Instructions: Complete the sentences below, using one of the words beginning with the letter "D" from the previous section. Note that some gaps require a single word, while others may need a phrasal verb or idiomatic expression. You may also need to change the form of the word. The answers are provided at the end of book.

1) A _____ cloud hung overhead, threatening us with rain.

2) The crime of murder is a _____ act.

3) Students must be _____ when filling in the answer sheet to be sure that they put the answers in the correct space.

4) The mechanic _____ the engine of the car in order to repair it.

5) His farm is very _____. He grows crops and also raises various types of animals.

6) Drugs are the _____ of many people, and addiction is a growing problem in our country.

7) There is a high level of _____ in their family. In fact, most of the siblings don't speak to each other.

8) That restaurant was so _____. It appeared that the floor had never been cleaned.

9) I know that you are about to panic, but please don't make a decision in _____.

10) The store was offering a refund to customers because of a _____ in the product they had sold.

Words – E

Instructions: Study the words below, paying attention to their meanings as well as how they are used in the example sentences. Then complete the exercise that follows.

earnest - (adj.) relating to sincerity in character. e.g. - If you are earnest when speaking about your problem, you will certainly receive support and sympathy. (n.) earnestness; (adv.) earnestly.

eerie - (adj.) frightening; scary. e.g. - Why do you watch those eerie movies? You know you always feel afraid afterwards. Der. (adv.) eerily.

effigy - (n.) a monument or memorial shaped in the likeness of a particular individual. e.g. - An effigy of Abraham Lincoln can be found in the center of Washington D.C.

elaborate - (adj.) developed; containing many details. e.g. - He told such an elaborate story that it was impossible to remember all the details. Der. (n.) elaboration; (v.) elaborate; (adv.) elaborately.

elated - (adj.) very pleased or happy; delighted. e.g. - She was elated when her baby was born. It was the happiest day of her life. Der. (n.) elation; (v.) elate.

elements - (n.) changes in the weather. e.g. - You must dress yourself warmly in the winter to protect yourself against the elements.

elicit - (v.) to bring out; evoke. e.g. - The teacher gave the students many clues in order to elicit the correct answer. Der. (n.) elicitation.

elite - (adj.) relating to a limited group; (syn.) exclusive. e.g. - The Beverly Hills Hotel is used only by an elite group of people, including famous movie stars.

elusive - (adj.) impossible to be accomplished or maintained. e.g. - Her dream of becoming a professional ballet dancer has proved to be elusive. She was rejected at the audition and is now working in a department store. Der. (n.) elusion; (n.) elusiveness; (v.) elude; (adv.) elusively.

ember - (n.) a small glowing fragment which remains when a fire is being extinguished. e.g. - Be careful when removing embers from your fireplace. They may still be burning and should not be thrown on paper garbage.

embezzle - (v.) to use one's own position to steal company money or property for personal use. e.g. - The company's accountant had been embezzling money for years by transferring it from the company's bank to his own personal account. Der. (n.) embezzlement; (adj.) embezzled.

embroil - (v.) to cause to become involved in a conflict. e.g. - She became embroiled in the argument by telling a different version of events.

eminent - (adj.) showing superiority or high achievement in one's profession. e.g. - The professor was eminent in the field of micro-biology and had written several well-known books on the subject.

emission - (n.) to give off or send out light, sound, or smell. e.g. The emission of poisonous gases into the atmosphere is illegal. Der. (v.) emit.

emulate - (v.) to imitate or equal in quality. e.g. - Your brother is a perfect child. You should try to emulate him. Der. (n.) emulation; (adj.) emulate.

encompass - (v.) to involve or include. (syn.) encompass. e.g. - Business Studies encompass the subjects of marketing and economics.

encounter - (v.) to meet or come across. e.g. - I encountered Jane in the shopping mall, although we hadn't arranged to meet. Der. (n.) encounter.

endeavor - (v.) to attempt with difficulty. e.g. - The doctor will endeavor to see you this afternoon, although his schedule is quite full. Der. (n.) endeavor.

endorse - (v.) to openly express approval or support; (syn.) back. e.g. - The budget reductions that the manager proposed were not endorsed by the company. Der. (n.) endorsement; (adj.) endorsed.

endowment - (n.) grant or contribution of money for support of an activity. e.g. - The millionaire contributed a substantial endowment towards the building of the new hospital. Der. (v.) endow; (adj.) endowed.

enervating - (adj.) exhausting. e.g. - Running a marathon is an enervating experience and requires several days of rest afterwards. Der. (n.) enervate.

engulf - (v.) to be consumed totally by fire. e.g. - The fire department could not save the building since it was already engulfed in flames when they arrived.

enhance - (v.) to make something greater or more beautiful. e.g. - Some people have plastic surgery in order to enhance their appearance. Der. (n.) enhancement; (adj.) enhanced.

enmity - (n.) hatred; (syn.) contempt. e.g. - They hardly parted as friends. In fact, I'd say she feels enmity towards him.

ensign - (n.) a flag which indicates nationality; (syn.) banner. e.g. - The ensign of the United States is red, white, and blue.

entail - (v.) to involve or include. e.g. - Sarah's new job as manager entails many responsibilities.

enterprise - (n.) a business organization established for a particular purpose or activity. e.g. - Banks and insurance companies are business enterprises. Der. (adj.) enterprising.

enthrall - (v.) to totally attract the attention of someone; to charm. e.g. - She was totally enthralled with the charm of the Hawaiian islands and would like to go there again next summer. Der. (adj.) enthralling; (n.) enthrallment.

entice - (v.) to attract by persuasion or influence. e.g. - The advertisement in the store window enticed him to go inside. Der. (n.) enticement; (adj.) enticing.

entity - (n.) a business or enterprise. e.g. - A partnership is one type of business entity.

entreat - (v.) to beg; (syn.) beseech; implore. e.g. - The organization entreated the public to give donations to charity. Der. (n.) entreaty.

equivocation - (n.) the action of speaking in a way that is likely to cause confusion or misunderstanding. e.g. - The lawyer spoke with equivocation, saying that the product was not dangerous, nor was it safe. Der. (v.) equivocate; (adj.) equivocal; (adv.) equivocally; (ant.) unequivocal.

era - (n.) a period in history. e.g. - The Middle Ages were a particular era in history.

erratic - (adj.) unpredictable; inconsistent. e.g. - Her moods are so erratic. You never know if she'll be happy or upset. Der. (adv.) erratically.

escort - (v.) to go along with; (syn.) accompany. e.g. - Rachel's father escorted her on her first date. She was so embarrassed to be seen with him. Der. (n.) escort.

esteem - (n.) value or appreciation. e.g. - You are totally lacking in self-esteem. You should really think more highly of yourself. Der. (v.) esteem.

estuary - (n.) the mouth of a river or other waterway. e.g. - The Mississippi River flows south to its estuary at the Gulf of Mexico.

eternal - (adj.) lasting forever. e.g. - Guess what? My boyfriend declared his eternal love for me last night. He said he'd love me forever. Der. (n.) eternity; (adv.) eternally.

exacerbate - (v.) to make worse or more severe. e.g. - He exacerbated the fire by throwing gasoline on it. Der. (n.) exacerbation.

exaggerate - (v.) to overstate in size or amount. e.g. - The fisherman exaggerated by saying that he had caught a twelve pound fish when, in fact, it weighed only six pounds. Der. (n.) exaggeration; (adj.) exaggerated; (adv.) exaggeratedly.

exalt - (v.) to give praise and glory. e.g. - The soldier was exalted for the bravery he displayed in battle.

exasperation - (n.) a state of extreme irritation or annoyance. e.g. - He felt exasperation when the building collapsed while he was just finishing the repairs. Der. (v.) exasperate; (adj.) exasperated, exasperating; (adv.) exasperatingly.

exclusive - (adj.) capable of use or possession only by a limited group. e.g. - The exclusive news report was broadcast only by one channel. Der. (n.) exclusivity; (v.) exclude; (adv.) exclusively.

exertion - (n.) excessive physical activity. e.g. - Much exertion was required to climb the mountain. Afterwards, the climbers were exhausted. Der. (v.) exert; (adj.) exerting.

exhale - (v.) to expel air out by breathing. e.g. - He exhaled the cigarette smoke by breathing it out of his nose and mouth. Der. (n.) exhalation.

exhaust - (n.) the expenditure of gas from a machine. e.g. - The exhaust from automobiles has caused environmental problems in all major European cities.

exile - (v.) to expel or force to leave, esp. one's country of origin. e.g. - She was exiled from government office due to her political viewpoints. Der. (n.) exile.

exonerate - (v.) to clear from accusation or responsibility. e.g. - A finding of "not guilty" exonerates a suspect from all responsibility for a crime. Der. (n.) exoneration.

exorbitant - (adj.) excessive in quantity or price; (syn.) extortionate. e.g. - You paid $5 for a candy bar. What an exorbitant price. Der. (n.) exorbitance; (adv.) exorbitantly.

expel - (v.) to force to leave school, usually for misbehavior. e.g. - He was expelled from high school for starting a fire in the classroom. Der. (n.) expulsion; (adj.) expelled.

exploit - (v.) to use or manipulate another person for one's own purposes. e.g. - Don't let him exploit you. He's only using you for money and a place to stay. Der. (n.) exploitation.

extenuating - (adj.) relating to lessening the seriousness of a charge; mitigating. e.g. - The use of self-defense is an extenuating circumstance against the charge of murder. Der. (v.) extenuate.

extermination - (n.) the action of killing insects or rodents. e.g. - After discovering several mice in our kitchen, it was necessary to call a company into our home for <u>extermination</u>. Der. (v.) exterminate.

extortionate - (adj.) excessively expensive; (syn.) exorbitant. e.g. - He paid the <u>extortionate</u> price of $5000 for a pair of tennis shoes. Der. (adv.) extortionately.

extract - (v.) to remove. e.g. - The information you need can be <u>extracted</u> from this book. Der. (n.) extract, extraction; (adj.) extracted.

extravagant - (adj.) unnecessarily high in price or expense. e.g. - Giving your girlfriend a new car for her birthday was too <u>extravagant</u>. You should have given her a much cheaper present. Der. (n.) extravagance.

Exercises – E

Instructions: Complete the sentences below, using one of the words beginning with the letter "E" from the previous section. Note that some gaps require a single word, while others may need a phrasal verb or idiomatic expression. You may also need to change the form of the word. The answers are provided at the end of book.

1) Success proved to be _____ to him, and he couldn't realize his dream of becoming a professional football player.

2) The last few weeks of the semester are _____. I get very little sleep because I am preparing so many assignments and essays.

3) The business _____ had corporate offices in the same building.

4) I know she is angry at you, but don't _____ the situation by telling her that she is foolish.

5) You can get an excused absence from class if there are _____ circumstances.

6) Preparing for a party _____ many small details.

7) An _____ of the man who founded the town can be found in the park.

8) That street has an _____ atmosphere after dark, and many people avoid it because they are afraid.

9) The manager was fired for _____ from the company bank account.

10) I will _____ to get into an advanced English class, although I may not succeed.

Words – F

Instructions: Study the words below, paying attention to their meanings as well as how they are used in the example sentences. Then complete the exercise that follows.

fable - (n.) a story based on magical happenings. e.g. - That story is a <u>fable</u> because it's not possible for a frog to turn into a handsome prince.

fabricate - (v.) manufacture; (syn.) assemble. e.g. - Alfonso <u>fabricated</u> a huge story which was made of lies. Der. (n.) fabrication; (adj.) fabricated.

face the music - (id.) to accept reality. e.g. - <u>Face the music</u>! Your girlfriend isn't coming back to you!

facetious - (adj.) relating to inappropriate humor or jokes. e.g. - When I said that Tom Cruise was my cousin, I was only being <u>facetious</u>. I never thought that you would take me seriously. Der. (adv.) facetiously.

fad - (n.) an attraction or fashion existing for a short period of time with overwhelming interest. e.g. - Bell-bottomed jeans were a <u>fad</u> in the 1960's.

fade - (v.) to gradually lose color. e.g. - Blue jeans <u>fade</u> after repeated washing and become lighter in color. Der. (adj.) faded.

fair-weather friend - (id.) loyal only during times of good fortune. e.g. - Don't trust him. He's a <u>fair-weather</u> friend.

fallacious - (adj.) incorrect as a result of being based on false theories or beliefs. e.g. - The theory that the earth is flat is totally <u>fallacious</u>. Der. (n.) fallacy; (adv.) fallaciously.

fatality - (n.) a death caused by an accident or natural disaster. e.g. - Three <u>fatalities</u> resulted from the road accident. A man, woman, and child were reported dead. Der. (adj.) fatal; (adv.) fatally.

fathom - (v.) to understand or comprehend, esp. with difficulty. e.g. - I can't <u>fathom</u> this chemistry homework. Can you explain it to me? Der. (adj.) fathomable; (ant.) unfathomable.

feat - (n.) accomplishment. e.g. - Receiving a university degree by the age of thirteen is quite an amazing <u>feat</u>.

feeble - (adj.) lacking in strength, esp. as a result of old age. e.g. - Anne's grandmother is quite <u>feeble</u> and cannot lift heavy objects. Der. (adv.) feebly.

feel together - (id.) to feel organized and well. e.g. - I wouldn't approach your boss for a raise today. She can't be feeling together after the way she drank at the party last night.

fellowship - (adj.) relating to the gathering of individual members in a group or society. e.g. - The fellowship of Veterans of Former Wars gathers once a month for a meeting in the town hall.

fertilizer - (n.) chemicals applied to planted fields to enhance growth and increase production. e.g. - Health conscious people prefer naturally-grown organic vegetables as they believe that the fertilizers placed on other vegetables are harmful to the health. Der. (v.) fertilize; (adj.) fertile; (adj.) fertilized.

fervid - (adj.) showing extreme enthusiasm or passion. e.g. - He is a fervid fan of the local baseball team. He never misses a game.

fetter - (v.)(met.) to restrict; to prevent the progress of. e.g. - Being the mother of four young children, she is fettered with responsibility. Der. (n.) fetter.

fib - (v.) to lie. e.g. - He fibbed about being related to the President. Der. (n.) fib.

fickle - (adj.) changeable or inconstant; capricious. e.g. - She is a very fickle girl and constantly changes her mind.

fidget - (v.) to sit restlessly. e.g. - Young children often fidget if they have been sitting in one place for too long. Der. (adj.) fidgeting.

figure - (v.)(met.) to think or believe; reckon. e.g. - I figure that he's lying because his story doesn't make sense.

figure – (1)(n.) the shape of a person's body; (2)(n.) amount; number. e.g. - (1) Your figure would be better if you went on a diet. (2) The latest figures indicate that the population of our city is now 10,000. Der. (v.) figure.

figure out - (ph. v.) to attempt to understand. e.g. - I can't figure out my math homework.

fizzle out - (id.) to reduce gradually in amount or quality. e.g. - Interest in our exercise class has fizzled out. There are only two students left.

flank - (v.) to be located on both sides of someone or something. e.g. - Our house is flanked by a grocery store on the east and a parking lot on the west.

flap - (n.) a piece of paper or cardboard which is placed over an adjoining piece. e.g. - You must moisten the flap in order to seal the back of the envelope.

flat broke - (id.) to be completely out of money. e.g. - Alan is flat broke and is considering filing for bankruptcy.

flaunt - (v.) to show or display something obviously or pretentiously. e.g. - She flaunted her new diamond ring by waving her hand in front of my face. Der. (adj.) flaunted.

flaw - (n.) an imperfection in appearance or function. e.g. - The jacket had a serious flaw since one sleeve was longer than the other. Der. (adj.) flawed.

flicker - (n.) a small flame. e.g. - The flicker from the candle provided enough light to see in the dark room. Der. (v.) flicker.

flinch - (v.) to experience involuntary spasms as a result of pain. e.g. - The man's legs flinched and jerked when they were crushed in the accident. Der. (n.) flinch.

flirt with disaster - (id.) to become involved in a dangerous or risky situation. e.g. - Every time you drive over the speed limit, you are just flirting with disaster.

flock - (n.) a group of animals, such as sheep or birds. e.g. - The flock of sheep was gathered at the north end of the field. Der. (v.) flock.

flog a dead horse - (id.) to talk too much about a situation that cannot be changed, causing others to become bored or fed up. e.g. - My classmate is always talking about failing her exams. She is flogging a dead horse.

flop - (n.)(met.) a complete and total lack of success. e.g. - His business was a flop because he didn't know how to manage his money.

flounder - (v.) to work without obtaining results; to struggle. e.g. - Chris really floundered during his first few weeks on the job since his boss did not provide any instructions or assistance. Der. (adj.) floundering.

flourish - (v.) to reach the highest state of activity or development. e.g. - Flowers flourish if they are grown in the warmth of a greenhouse.

fluctuate - (v.) to change back and forth. e.g. - The weather often fluctuates from hot to cold at this time of year. Der. (n.) fluctuation.

fodder - (n.) animal food. e.g. - The horse was in the stable, eating his fodder.

foil - (v.) to thwart or prevent the progress of. e.g. - The bank robber's plan was foiled when the security alarm went off. Der. (adj.) foiled.

folklore - (n.) traditional stories. e.g.- Some books are based on fact. Others are based on folklore.

fondle - (v.) to stroke gently; (syn.) pet. e.g. - She fondled the cat as it slept on the sofa.

for all intents and purposes - (id.) for all practical purposes; in effect. e.g. - My computer is useless for all intents and purposes since I cannot use new software on it.

for keeps - (id.) to take possession or ownership of sthg forever. e.g. - He gave me a diamond ring for keeps.

forage - (v.) to search for something, esp. in the countryside. e.g. - She was foraging in her disorganized closet, looking for her favorite pair of shoes.

forecast - (v.) to predict; to estimate. e.g. - The meteorologist forecasts snow for tomorrow. Der. (n.) forecast.

foremost - (adj.) the most important or noteworthy. e.g. - First and foremost, you must always be honest.

forerunner - (n.) current authority or leader. e.g. - Coca-Cola is a forerunner in the soft drink industry.

forlorn - (adj.) loneliness and despair; (syn.) desolate. e.g. - He felt forlorn after his wife filed for divorce. Der. (n.) forlornness; (adv.) forlornly.

fortitude - (n.) strength; courage. e.g. - He showed great fortitude in saving the drowning man from the raging river. Der. (v.) fortify; (adj.) fortified.

fortuitous - (adj.) happening by chance or accident; unplanned. e.g. - I had a fortuitous meeting with an old friend today. By coincidence, we both happened to be in the doctor's office at the same time. Der. (adv.) fortuitously.

foster - (v.) to adopt or encourage; nurture. e.g. - You'd feel more optimistic if you fostered a positive attitude.

fraction - (n.) a part or percentage of the whole. e.g. - He ate only a fraction of the pie. Three-quarters of it is left. Der. (v.) fractionalize; (adj.) fractional; (adv.) fractionally.

fracture - (n.) a broken bone. e.g. - Tom had many fractures as a result of the car accident. Der. (v.) fracture; (adj.) fractured.

frail - (adj.) being easily broken; weak. e.g. - Elderly people suffer from frail bones that can break easily. Der. (n.) frailty; (adv.) frailly.

fraudulent - (adj.) based on trickery or dishonesty. e.g. - His offer to make you president of his company is entirely fraudulent since no such company exists. Der. (n.) fraud; (adv.) fraudulently.

fraught - (adj.) to be full of something. e.g. - He is fraught with nervousness these days about his upcoming wedding.

fresh out of sthg - (id.) to have exhausted the supply of something. e.g. - We are fresh out of grapefruit today ma'am. You'll need to come back again tomorrow.

fret - (v.) to be anxious with worry. e.g. - Joanne has been fretting about her exam results. She is worried that she might have failed. Der. (n.) fret.

frigid - (adj.) extremely cold; freezing. e.g. - The frigid weather caused the plants to freeze. Der. (n.) frigidity; (adv.) frigidly.

frivolous - (adj.) without seriousness or importance. e.g. - Don't you think it was frivolous of her to complain about losing such a small amount of money?

frolic - (v.) to run and play freely. e.g. - The children were frolicking in the playground. Der. (n.) frolic; (adj.) frolicsome.

frontier - (n.) an unclaimed or unsettled area or territory. e.g. - Outer space is an unexplored frontier

frugal - (adj.) to be very restrictive with money or in spending. e.g. - Isabel is very frugal as she is living on a pension.

fruitful - (adj.) relating to something which is very productive. e.g. - I had a fruitful afternoon at the office. I finished all of my work. Der. (adv.) fruitfully.

fugitive - (n.) an individual who has escaped or is running from the law. e.g. - Charles escaped from prison five years ago and now lives his life hiding as a fugitive.

fulsome - (adj.) abundant or excessive. e.g. - He received fulsome praise for returning the lost ten dollars. Der. (n.) fulsomeness; (adv.) fulsomely.

fumbling - (adj.) failing to obtain the desired result; (syn.) floundering. e.g. - He made many fumbling attempts, but was never successful. Der. (v.) fumble.

fume - (1)(n.) vapor; (syn.) exhaust; (2)(met.)(v.) to be very angry. e.g. (1) - The odor from this paint is so strong that I am getting a headache from the fumes. (2) He was fuming after I insulted him.

fundamental - (adj.) basic; (syn.) rudimentary. e.g. - The law of gravity is one of the fundamental rules of physics. Der. (adv.) fundamentally.

Exercises – F

Instructions: Complete the sentences below, using one of the words beginning with the letter "F" from the previous section. Note that some gaps require a single word, while others may need a phrasal verb or idiomatic expression. You may also need to change the form of the word. The answers are provided at the end of book.

1) She was being _____. She didn't mean what she said.

2) The soldier was _____ by a comrade on his right and another on his left.

3) I had a _____ encounter with my cousin at the mall today. It was such a coincidence. I didn't even know she was going shopping.

4) It is _____ to complain about such a small, insignificant problem.

5) The _____ principles of geometry state that a right angle will always have ninety degrees.

6) The orchestra paid _____ tribute to the composer by playing all of his concertos.

7) Children _____ if given love, care, discipline, and support.

8) Our plans for vacation were _____ when a hurricane hit the resort area.

9) The horses were _____ in the field, running around playfully with one another.

10) Attendance at yoga will _____ if the instructor fails to make the class interesting or useful.

Words – G to H

Instructions: Study the words below, paying attention to their meanings as well as how they are used in the example sentences. Then complete the exercise that follows.

gait - (n.) an individual's style of running, walking, or stepping. e.g. - He finished the race first because he ran with the fastest gait.

garbled - (adj.) confused or unclear in meaning. e.g. - He left a garbled message that no one could understand. Der. (v.) garble.

garish - (adj.) the quality of being displayed excessively or tastelessly. e.g. - The interior decorations of their house were garish: red carpeting, orange curtains, and a purple sofa. Der. (adv.) garishly.

garnish - (n.) fruit or vegetable pieces added to food or drinks to enhance their appearance. e.g. - Slices of lemon or orange are used as garnishes for dishes served in restaurants. Der. (v.) garnish.

garrulous - (adj.) talkative; outgoing; (syn.) gregarious, ebullient. e.g. - He is so garrulous that sometimes it's difficult to make him stop talking. Der. (adv.) garrulously.

gash - (n.) a long, deep cut. e.g. - He got a gash on his finger when the knife he was using to cut the cheese slipped from his hand. Der. (v.) gash.

gauge - (n.) a small machine which is used for measuring. e.g. - The gauge on this machine will measure the air pressure inside the tires. Der. (v.) gauge.

gear (towards) - (v.) to make to satisfy a certain condition. e.g. - The style of clothes in that store is geared towards teenagers. You won't be able to find a gift for your mother there. Der. (n.) gear.

genial - (adj.) polite, well-mannered. e.g. - He is very genial. Not once have I heard him speak in a rude or impolite way. Der. (adv.) genially.

get along like cats and dogs - (id.) to be entirely incompatible. e.g. - I can't live with my mother. We get along like cats and dogs.

get in touch - (id.) to get in contact with someone. e.g. - Get in touch with me next week. You can telephone me at home.

get on sbdy's good side - (id.) to win someone's favor. e.g. - He tried to get on the teacher's good side by bringing her gifts.

get the lowdown on something - (id.) to obtain secret or inside information about something. e.g. - Did you get the lowdown? I heard a rumor that the plant is going to close.

gimmick - (n.) a trick or feature used to attract to attention. e.g. - Free gifts or samples are often included with new products as a gimmick to entice the customer to buy them.

give sbdy a lift - (id.) to give someone a ride in your car. e.g. - Can you give me a lift into town?

give sbdy the creeps - (id.) to frighten someone. e.g. - Horror movies give me the creeps.

give sbdy a break - (id.) to stop giving harsh treatment to an individual. e.g. - What do you mean? You won't help me! Give me a break!

glum - (adj.) without hope; depressed. e.g. - Bruce is really glum these days. He is unhappy about failing his exams again. Der. (adv.) glumly.

gnaw - (v.) to chew on, esp. continuously. e.g. - The rats were gnawing on the wood with their teeth.

go-ahead - (n.) a gesture of authority or approval. e.g. - After weeks of refusing, the manager finally gave the go-ahead for the project.

gobble - (v.) to eat quickly or greedily. e.g. - He gobbled the food like a pig and got a stomach ache from eating so quickly.

go-between - (n.) an individual who makes arrangements or mediates. e.g. - He acted as a go-between in arranging the blind date for his two friends. Der. (ph. v.) go between.

gorgeous - (adj.) very beautiful; stunning. e.g. - The winner of the beauty contest was a very gorgeous woman.

grab a bite - (id.) to go for a meal, esp. quickly. e.g. - Let's grab a bite for lunch.

grain - (n.) seeds of cereal plants, such as corn or wheat. e.g. - Food products such as rice and corn are grains.

grasp - (1)(v.) to hold or embrace with the hands or arms; (syn.) clasp, clutch; (2)(met.) to understand. e.g. - (1) Mary stood at the bus stop, grasping her bags in her hands. (2) I can't grasp what you are saying. Can you please explain it to me again? Der. (n.) grasp.

grasping at straws - (id.) to try many alternative solutions in desperation. e.g. - You don't know the answer to the homework so now you're grasping at straws.

graze - (v.) to feed on grass. e.g. - The sheep were grazing in the meadow, eating grass.

green - (id.) inexperienced; without knowledge. e.g. – The new employee is green since today is his first day on the job, and he has no previous experience.

grimy - (adj.) dirty; filthy. e.g. - They live like pigs. Their house is so grimy. Der. (n.) grime.

grove - (n.) a small group of trees, which often bear fruit or nuts. e.g. - We have a small grove of pine trees in our front yard.

grow on - (id.) to get used to. e.g. - I didn't like my new school too much at first, but it has started to grow on me.

grumble - (v.) to complain; (syn.) whine. e.g. - There is no reason to grumble about your job. If you don't like it, find a new one. Der. (n.) grumble.

haggle (with) - (v.) to engage in discussions with buyers or sellers in order to agree upon a price; negotiate. e.g. - He haggled with the car salesman in order to negotiate a good price.

hamlet - (n.) a small town or village. e.g. - Two-hundred years ago, Chicago was a small hamlet, but now it's a huge city.

handle sthg - (id.) to endure or tolerate something. e.g. - I just can't handle waking up so early in the morning.

handy - (adj.) near at hand; easy to use; convenient. e.g. - The neighborhood convenience store is handy because it's very close to our house.

happy-go-lucky - (id.) carefree. e.g. - He's so happy-go-lucky that you'd think he didn't have a care in the world.

harvest - (v.) to gather produce from a field. e.g. - The farmer harvested the apples in the fall by picking them from the trees. Der. (n.) harvest.

haughty - (adj.) overly proud. e.g. - She was haughty about winning first prize in the contest. Der. (adv.) haughtily.

haunted - (adj.) relating to places that are believed to be occupied by ghosts or spirits of the dead. e.g. - Many people believe that spirits of the dead haunt graveyards. Der. (v.) haunt.

have a one-track mind - (id.) to only have one thing on your mind. e.g. - She has a one-track mind. All she ever thinks about is money.

have pull - (id.) to be influential. e.g. - I think he can get us tickets for the game on Sunday. He has pull with the team.

He made his bed, and now he can lie in it. - (id.) a person must face the consequences of his or her actions. e.g. - It was his own decision to cheat on the exam. Now that he got caught, I can only say that he made his bed, and now he can lie in it.

heard it through the grapevine - (id.) to hear some people talking or gossiping about a subject. e.g. - I wasn't told the news about the situation directly. I heard it through the grapevine.

hearth - (n.) the floor of a fireplace. e.g. - The fire was burning in the hearth.

hearty - (adj.) relating to physical strength and good health; (syn.) strapping. e.g. - Regular exercise and healthy food will make you hearty. Der. (n.) heartiness; (adv.) heartily.

hectic - (adj.) exceptionally active or busy. e.g. - What a hectic day. I haven't had a moment to rest. Der. (adv.) hectically.

heinous - (adj.) exceptionally shocking or horrible. e.g. - The murder of the young children was a heinous crime and should be punished severely.

hilarious - (adj.) very funny or humorous. e.g. - She told a hilarious story, which caused everyone to break out into fits of laughter. Der. (n.) hilarity; (adv.) hilariously.

hindrance - (n.) the action of holding back, delaying, or preventing the progress of something; (syn.) obstacle; stumbling block. e.g. - His constant interruptions were a hindrance to the completion of the job. Der. (v.) hinder.

hindsight - (n.) the understanding of the consequences of an event after it has occurred. e.g. - With hindsight, he realizes the mistakes he has made in his past.

hit the nail on the head - (id.) to make an appropriate remark or statement. e.g. - The politician hit the nail on the head when he said that more financial aid should be offered to students.

Hit the road! - (id.) Go away. Leave me alone. (syn.) Take a hike! e.g. - A strange man was bothering me in the mall so I told him to hit the road.

hit the spot - (id.) That was just what I was craving. e.g. - Lemonade really hits the spot on a hot summer day.

hoarse - (adj.) unpleasant or rough in sound. e.g. – My brother is hoarse from shouting too much at the football game last night. Der. (adv.) hoarsely.

hoax - (n.) a fictitious report of a sighting or event. e.g. - His report of viewing an aircraft from outer-space was a total hoax.

hold a grudge - (id.) to bear resentment towards another person. e.g. - Julia is still holding a grudge because I criticized her work.

hold your tongue - (id.) to keep one's opinions to oneself. e.g. - I wanted to tell her off, but I held my tongue.

holding the bag - (id.) to be forced to take an action or make a decision. e.g. - Kevin didn't help me as he promised and left me holding the bag.

hollow - (adj.) relating to objects that are not solid in content. e.g. - The children were disappointed that the candy was hollow and did not have a filling in the center. Der. (n.) hollow, hollowness; (v.) hollow; (adv.) hollowly.

hop in - (id.) get inside my car. e.g. - I'll take you to the store. Hop in.

How come? - (id.) Why? e.g. - She's not going out tonight. How come?

hunch - (n.) an instinctive feeling or idea. e.g. - I didn't have any proof that he was lying. It was only a hunch.

hurl - (v.) to throw with great force or strength. e.g. - The baseball player hurled the ball to his teammate, who caught it.

hushed - (adj.) quiet; subdued. e.g. - The examination hall was hushed as the students were writing. It was so quiet that you could hear a pin drop. Der. (v.) hush. Der. (n.) hush.

Exercises – G to H

Instructions: Complete the sentences below, using one of the words beginning with the letters "G" or "H" from the previous section. Note that some gaps require a single word, while others may need a phrasal verb or idiomatic expression. You may also need to change the form of the word. The answers are provided at the end of book.

1) If you should have any questions or complaints, please _____ with the manager of the company.

2) Parsley or mint are often used as _____ for meat dishes.

3) The daycare center is _____ because it's less than a mile from my home.

4) She _____ constantly about her boyfriend. If she is so unhappy, she should leave him.

5) You don't know how to respond to the accusation, so now you are _____.

6) If you shout too much you will become _____.

7) That meal really _____. I was craving a pizza.

8) The police officer didn't have any evidence to charge the suspect with the crime. He only had a _____.

9) The instructions were _____ , so we couldn't understand what we needed to do.

10) The auditorium was _____ as the Dean was about to begin her speech.

Words – I

Instructions: Study the words below, paying attention to their meanings as well as how they are used in the example sentences. Then complete the exercise that follows.

idle - (adj.) inactive or non-functioning. e.g. - The plant is closed because it is idle this month.

ignite - (v.) to start a fire. e.g. - The police investigation determined that the fire had been ignited with gasoline. Der. (n.) ignition.

illicit - (adj.) illegal. e.g. - Illicit drugs, such as heroin and cocaine, have become a serious problem of modern society. Der. (adv.) illicitly.

immaculate - (adj.) exceptionally clean or tidy. e.g. - Her house was so immaculate that no dust or dirt could be seen. Der. (adv.) immaculately.

immature - (adj.) childish. e.g. - Although my brother is 50 years old, he is immature and behaves like a child. Der. (n.) immaturity; (ant.) mature.

immense - (adj.) huge or extensive. e.g. - You wrote a 2,000 page book. That must have required an immense amount of work. Der. (adv.) immensely.

impact - (n.) effect; consequence. e.g. - Your failure to work hard now will have a negative impact on your future. Der. (v.) impact.

impartial - (adj.) relating to treatment with fairness and equality; unbiased. e.g. - An impartial teacher does not have favorite students, but treats all students equally. Der. (n.) impartiality; (adv.) impartially.

impeccable - (adj.) without fault or blame; perfect. e.g. - I don't believe his behavior is as impeccable as you say. Nobody's perfect, you know. Der. (adv.) impeccably.

imperative - (adj.) essential; exceptionally urgent or important. e.g. - It is imperative that this medicine be taken exactly every eight hours. Failure to do so can result in death.

implement - (n.) a tool or piece of equipment used for a specific purpose. e.g. - Several implements, such as plows, are needed to harvest crops from the fields in the fall. Der. (n.) implementation; (v.) implement.

implicate - (v.) to show proof of the commission of or involvement in a crime; (syn.) incriminate. e.g. - His possession of the gun used in the murder implicated him in the crime. Der. (n.) implication.

implore - (v.) to beg; (syn.) entreat, beseech. e.g. - The President <u>implored</u> the nation for their support during the country's economic crisis. Der. (adj.) imploring; (adv.) imploringly.

imposing - (adj.) overwhelming in size or amount. e.g. - A New York penthouse suite can cost well over $1,000,000, which is far too <u>imposing</u> for most people. Der. (v.) impose.

impregnable - (adj.) incapable of being entered or penetrated. e.g. - The castle was <u>impregnable</u> and could not be invaded by the enemy. Der. (n.) impregnability; (adv.) impregnably.

impropriety - (n.) improper behavior. e.g. - I can't believe you had the <u>impropriety</u> to flirt with your boss's wife. Der. (ant.) propriety.

in the red - (id.) to have a negative numerical balance. e.g. - The company had to close down after operating <u>in the red</u> for months.

incidental - (adj.) not relating to the main part; minor. e.g. - Your comments are only <u>incidental</u> and will not have an effect on our final decision. Der. (adv.) incidentally.

incongruity - (n.) incompatibility or disagreement between or among things. e.g. - There is total <u>incongruity</u> between the lies he told and reality. Der. (adj.) incongruous; (ant.) congruity.

incriminate - (v.) to show proof concerning the commission of or involvement in a crime; (syn.) implicate. e.g. - The presence of the attacker's blood type at the murder scene <u>incriminated</u> him in the crime. Der. (n.) incrimination; (adj.) incriminating.

indefatigable - (adj.) incapable of experiencing fatigue or exhaustion. e.g. - My boss is <u>indefatigable</u>. He never gets tired and is always energetic. Der. (adv.) indefatigably.

indigent - (adj.) living in conditions of poverty. e.g. - Without a home or a job, she is <u>indigent</u> and is living on the streets. Der. (n.) indigence.

indignant - (adj.) feeling anger as a result of being unfairly accused of a wrongdoing. e.g. - He became <u>indignant</u> when his wife wrongly accused him of cheating on her. Der. (n.) indignity; (adv.) indignantly.

indispensable - (adj.) essential; necessary. e.g. - Fresh food and water are <u>indispensable</u> for human survival. Der. (n.) indispensability; (adv.) indispensably.

indulge - (v.) to enjoy sthg without discipline, control, or restraint. e.g. - If you <u>indulge</u> in too much food, you will become fat. Der. (n.) indulgence; (adj.) indulgent; (adv.) indulgently.

industrious - (adj.) relating to very hard-working individuals. e.g. – The manager received a promotion because he was so industrious.

infirmity - (n.) the condition of being weak as a result of illness, injury, or disease. e.g. - His broken leg has never healed properly. This infirmity causes him great pain, especially when walking. Der. (adj.) infirm.

infringement - (n.)(syn.) violation. e.g. - Cheating on examinations is an infringement of the rules of this college. Der. (v.) infringe.

infuriate - (v.) to cause to become extremely angry. e.g. - Your comment that I am stupid really infuriates me! Der. (n.) fury; (adj.) furious.

ingenious - (adj.) exceptionally intelligent, intellectual, or inventive. e.g. - Men such as Einstein and Edison were highly ingenious.

inhabitant - (n.) resident. e.g. - He has been an inhabitant of Boston for the past fifteen years. Der. (v.) inhabit.

inhale - (v.) to draw air in by breathing. e.g. - He inhaled the cigarette smoke deep into his lungs. Der. (n.) inhalation.

inheritance - (n.) the action of receiving money or specific property upon another person's death. e.g. - James received a substantial inheritance when his parents died, and he is now quite rich. Der. (v.) inherit.

inimical - (adj.) harmful or adverse; hostile. e.g. - The United Nations attempts to improve inimical relationships among various countries through goodwill and diplomacy. Der. (adv.) inimically.

innate - (adj.) inborn; inherent. e.g. - She has innate musical talent and learned how to play the piano in only two days. Der. (adv.) innately.

innocuous - (adj.) not causing harm or injury. e.g. - That snake is not poisonous. In fact, it is totally innocuous.

innovative - (adj.) new; novel. e.g. - This innovative machine is bound to replace every similar older machine currently on the market. Der. (n.) innovation; (v.) innovate.

inquisition - (n.) the process of subjecting to questioning, esp. extensively; (syn.) interrogation. e.g. - Your mother subjected me to an inquisition. I have never been asked so many questions in my life. Der. (adj.) inquisitive; (adv.) inquisitively.

insinuation - (n.) sthg that is implied, inferred, or expressed indirectly. e.g. - His insinuation in saying that I never attended college was that I was stupid. Der. (v.) insinuate.

insolent - (adj.) exhibiting a lack of respect; impudent. e.g. - The insolent student told the teacher that he was stupid. Der. (n.) insolence.

inspiration - (n.) the action of receiving a profound influence, esp. of a spiritual or creative nature. e.g. - The love and support of her husband were an inspiration to her and helped her to write several romance novels. Der. (v.) inspire; (adj.) inspired, inspiring.

installation - (n.) the action of preparing something for use by setting it up in the designated place. e.g. - The installation of your dishwasher is best handled by a plumber. Der. (v.) install.

instigate - (v.) to cause or incite improper or destructive behavior. e.g. - The leader of the gang instigated his followers into starting the riot. Der. (n.) instigation.

insulation - (1)(n.) the action of preventing the discharge of electricity or loss of heat; (2)(n.)(met.) - the action of offering an individual protection from the consequences of their actions. e.g. - (1) Insulation was placed in the walls of the building in order to ensure warmth in the winter. (2) The criminal received insulation from liability after offering a bribe to the judge. Der. (v.) insulate; (adj.) insulated.

insuperable - (adj.) incapable of being surpassed or overcome; (syn.) insurmountable. e.g. - The problem with this computer system is insuperable. We have no choice but to abandon it and start over from the beginning. Der. (adv.) insuperably.

insurmountable - (adj.) incapable of being passed or overcome; (syn.) insuperable. e.g. - His problems seemed insurmountable and in desperation, he felt that he could not go on. Der. (adv.) insurmountably.

interrogation - (n.) questioning; (syn.) inquisition. e.g. - A full interrogation was conducted to determine the whereabouts of the stolen diamond. Der. (v.) interrogate.

intertwine (with) - (v.)(met.) to become mutually involved in. e.g. - He became intertwined with crime when he agreed to participate in the robbery.

intrepid - (adj.) brave; courageous; unafraid. e.g. - The intrepid explorers entered the cave in darkness. Der. (n.) intrepidity, intrepidness; (adv.) intrepidly.

intricate - (adj.) very detailed or complicated. e.g. - Advanced mathematics involves many intricate theories and calculations. Der. (adv.) intricately.

intrigue - (n.) a secret plan or scheme. e.g. - The political intrigue involved a plan to spy on enemy governments. Der. (v.) intrigue; (adj.) intriguing; (adv.) intriguingly.

inundate - (v.) to overwhelm or overpower. e.g. - The area was inundated with rain in the thunderstorm last night. Der. (n.) inundation.

invigorate - (v.) to provide energy; to stimulate. e.g. - Jogging in the fresh air always invigorates me. Der. (n.) invigoration; (adj.) invigorating; (adj.) invigorated.

irrevocable - (adj.) impossible to be changed, altered, or taken away. e.g. - Once you sign this agreement, it is irrevocable and cannot be changed in any way. Der. (adv.) irrevocably; (ant.) revocable.

It doesn't hold water - (id.) it's not believable. e.g. - I don't believe him. His story doesn't hold water.

It was a hit - (id.) it was very popular or a huge success. e.g. - The rock group's new song was a hit.

It was a piece of cake - (id.) it was very easy. e.g. - The exam was a piece of cake. I'm sure I passed.

It's old hat - (id.) it's old news. e.g. - Everyone knows that. It's old hat.

Exercises – I

Instructions: Complete the sentences below, using one of the words beginning with the letter "I" from the previous section. Note that some gaps require a single word, while others may need a phrasal verb or idiomatic expression. You may also need to change the form of the word. The answers are provided at the end of book.

1) Her tablecloth is always _____. There is never any spot or stain.

2) She was _____ in the robbery because she had some of the stolen money in her bag.

3) The business was _____ for two years and finally had to close down.

4) She has been an _____ of the State of Arizona for ten years.

5) Her English is _____. Her vocabulary is precise, and her grammar is always correct.

6) The political leader _____ a rebellion against the government.

7) He is always _____. He is lazy and never gets anything done.

8) The teacher _____ the students to pay attention in class.

9) Magellan was an _____ explorer. He travelled to many parts of the world without having a rest or taking a break.

10) Working hard will have a positive _____ on your future career.

Words J to L

Instructions: Study the words below, paying attention to their meanings as well as how they are used in the example sentences. Then complete the exercise that follows.

jagged - (adj.) consisting of cut or broken edges. e.g. - The attacker threatened to cut his victim with the jagged edge of a broken bottle. Der. (n.) jaggedness; (adv.) jaggedly.

jeer - (v.) to tease or taunt; to subject to ridicule. e.g. - The cruel children jeered at the overweight boy, calling him "fatty." Der. (n.) jeer; (adj.) jeering; (adv.) jeeringly.

jeopardize - (v.) to risk or endanger. e.g. - You will jeopardize your health if you continue smoking so much. Der. (n.) jeopardy.

jot down - (id.) to write quickly in note form. e.g. - He jotted down the number that his friend gave him over the telephone.

jumbled - (adj.) disorderly or disorganized state; (syn.) cluttered. e.g. - The child's toys were laying in a jumbled pile in the corner of the room. Der. (n.) jumble; (v.) jumble.

jurisdiction - (n.) the authority to administer and apply laws and regulations. e.g. - The local sheriff has jurisdiction over this town.

keep in touch - (id.) to stay in contact with someone through telephone calls or correspondence. e.g. - Although my best friend lives miles away, we still manage to keep in touch.

Keep it down! - (id.) Be quiet! e.g. - Keep it down in there! I'm trying to study!

keep sbdy posted - (id.) to keep someone informed. e.g. - We expect to hear some news next week, so we'll keep you posted.

keep the lid on it - (id.) to keep something a secret. e.g. - I'll tell you a secret if you can keep the lid on it.

kernel - (1)(n.) a single seed from an ear of corn; (2)(met.) the basic or essential part. e.g. - (1) Kernels of corn are heated in oil to make popcorn; (2) The kernel of his argument was that I was lying.

kettle - (n.) a large metal container used for the purpose of cooking. e.g. - The macaroni was placed in the water boiling in the kettle.

knack - (n.) talent. e.g. - He has a knack for playing the guitar.

label - (n.) a piece of paper or plastic placed on an item for purposes of identifying its contents. e.g. - The label on the suitcase gave the name and address of its owner. Der. (v.) label.

lag - (v.) to become delayed or fall behind. e.g. - The race was close at the beginning, but the first runner won when the second runner lagged behind.

land - (v.) to find or locate. e.g. - You should be able to land a job. There are hundreds of employment opportunities listed in the newspaper advertisements.

lark - (n.) something done impulsively for fun or amusement. e.g. - We suddenly decided to go to the movies on a lark. Der. (ph. v.) lark about.

lash - (v.) to strike or hit, esp. with a whip or stick. e.g. - Slaves were often lashed with whips by their masters. This often caused their skin to become red or to bleed. Der. (n.) lash.

lassitude - (n.) tiredness; exhaustion. e.g. - The marathon runner showed great lassitude after finishing the race and rested on the grass nearby.

latent - (adj.) hidden; not obvious or visible. e.g. - The refrigerator had a latent defect that could not be discovered, even through careful examination. Der. (adv.) latently; (ant.) patent.

laud - (n.) praise; honor. e.g. He graduated at the top of his class and received laud on graduation day. Der. (v.) laud; (adj.) laudable; (adv.) laudably.

layperson - (n.) an individual possessing common knowledge on a certain subject; non-professional; non-expert. e.g. - He is a layperson on the subject of computers. He has no education or qualifications in that area.

ledge - (n.) a narrow shelf which sticks out from a wall of building. e.g. - Many birds were sitting outside on the high ledge of the building.

lenient - (adj.) easy-going about or accepting of the improper behavior of another person. e.g. - Mary's mother is so lenient. She lets her do whatever she wants. Der. (n.) lenience.

let it slip - (id.) to divulge secret information. e.g. - That was supposed to be a secret, but he let it slip.

let the cat out of the bag - (id.) to divulge secret information. e.g. - I told her not to tell anyone, but she let the cat out of the bag.

liability - (n.) responsibility or obligation according to the law. e.g. - Debts which are owed to others are considered liabilities. Der. (adj.) liable.

licentious - (adj.) offensive in content or lacking in morality; (syn.) vulgar; lewd. e.g. - Movies with licentious subjects may only be seen by adults. Due to their sexual content, these films may not be seen by children.

lighten up - (id.) to relax. e.g. - You'd better learn to lighten up or you'll have a heart attack.

like looking for a needle in a haystack - (id.) to search for something that has many possible locations. e.g. - Searching for our lost keys on the beach was like looking for a needle in a haystack.

limb - (n.) an arm or leg of a human being. e.g. - You'll risk life and limb if you attempt to cross that busy street during rush hour.

limp - (n.) to walk unevenly, favoring one leg over another. e.g. - Pedro's broken leg did not heal properly, and he now walks with a limp. Der. (v.) limp.

linger - (v.) to remain or delay departure. e.g. - Fatima lingered at my house, talking until 2:00 a.m., although she intended to have left earlier.

livelihood - (n.) method of providing financial support for an individual's existence. e.g. - He makes his livelihood by working as a clerk in a grocery store.

livestock - (n.) animals which are raised for sale. e.g. - The livestock raised on many farms consists of cows and pigs.

livid - (adj.) angry or furious. e.g. - He was livid when I told him he was stupid and lazy. Der. (n.) lividity.

loathe - (v.) to hate or despise. e.g. - I loathe waking up early in the morning. I really can't stand it. Der. (n.) loathing; (adj.) loath, loathsome.

loiter - (v.) to remain in a place without any obvious purpose. e.g.- The youngsters were just loitering at the convenience store. They had no real interest in buying anything.

loot - (v.) to seize objects during a robbery or war; (syn.) pillage, plunder. e.g. - The thieves looted the store, taking TVs, stereos, and microwave ovens. Der. (n.) loot; (adj.) looted.

loquacious - (adj.) eloquent or excessive in speech. e.g. - The loquacious principal gave a two-hour speech at the graduation ceremony. Der. (n.) loquacity; (adv.) loquaciously.

lousy - (adj.) very poor; miserable. e.g. - I feel lousy today. I think I'm going to be sick.

lucrative - (adj.) relating to the production of great wealth or profit. e.g. - He was able to retire early as a result of the large sum of money he had made from lucrative investments. Der. (adv.) lucratively.

lukewarm - (adj.) being neither hot nor cold; (syn.) tepid. e.g. - I like to bathe in lukewarm water in order not to feel too hot or too cold.

lunatic - (n.) a crazy person. e.g. - He is acting like a lunatic lately. I think he's gone crazy. Der. (n.) lunacy.

lurch - (v.) to suddenly change course or direction. e.g. - The car suddenly lurched off the road and crashed into a tree.

lure - (v.) to attract or entice. e.g. - He was lured into buying the car by its low price. Der. (n.) lure.

lurk - (v.) to wait secretly in a place for the purpose of doing harm. e.g. - The criminal was lurking in the shadows, waiting to rob the old lady.

lush - (adj.) abundant in grass and greenery. e.g. - The beautiful, lush garden had plentiful grass and flowers. Der. (n.) lushness; (adv.) lushly.

luxurious - (adj.) providing an expensive and rich environment, beyond what is necessary. e.g. - The king lived a luxurious lifestyle in a palace decorated with gold. Der. (n.) luxury; (adv.) luxuriously.

Exercises – J to L

Instructions: Complete the sentences below, using one of the words beginning with the letters "J" to "L" from the previous section. Note that some gaps require a single word, while others may need a phrasal verb or idiomatic expression. You may also need to change the form of the word. The answers are provided at the end of book.

1) He _____ the address using a pen and paper.

2) The cause of certain health conditions is sometimes _____ and cannot be discovered through examinations or tests.

3) The _____ speaker gave a presentation that lasted for ninety minutes.

4) She has a _____ for music. She can sing and play the piano.

5) The clothes were in a _____ on top of the bed. She need to fold them and put them away.

6) The _____ on the package stated the nutritional information.

7) The billionaire had a _____ home that had thirty-five rooms.

8) Businesses have many _____ and other debts to be paid.

9) That magazine is _____. It may only be seen by adults.

10) The judge has _____ over the proceedings in the case.

Words – M to O

Instructions: Study the words below, paying attention to their meanings as well as how they are used in the example sentences. Then complete the exercise that follows.

magnanimity - (n.) generosity. e.g. - The wealthy family showed great magnanimity in donating such a large sum of money to charity. Der. (adj.) magnanimous; (adv.) magnanimously.

magnify - (v.) to make larger. e.g. – My grandmother's vision is quite bad. She can read the newspaper only with a special glass that magnifies the letters. Der. (n.) magnification; (adj.) magnifying.

make heads or tails of sthg - (id.) to attempt to understand something with difficulty. e.g. - I can't make heads or tails of this map. Do you know which road to take?

make the big time - (id.) the highest level of success of a project or venture. e.g. - An actor is considered to have made the big time when he stars in a leading role.

make the grade - (id.) to have an acceptable standard of performance. e.g. - I didn't get to play in the game because I couldn't make the grade.

make yourself scarce - (id.) to avoid friends because of a situation which has caused conflict. e.g. - I haven't seen Jodi in weeks. She has made herself scarce.

malice - (n.) the desire to inflict harm, esp. when caused by feelings of hatred. e.g. - The victims feel great malice towards their attacker and hope that he receives the death penalty. Der. (adj.) malicious; (adv.) maliciously.

mandatory - (adj.) required; necessary; obligatory; (syn.) compulsory. e.g. - Completion of this form is mandatory. It must be filled in by every applicant.

manifest - (v.) to show or display obviously. e.g. - The disease manifests itself as fever and weakness. Der. (n.) manifestation; (adv.) manifestly.

manifold - (adj.) consisting of a wide variety; many. e.g. - She had manifold reasons for resigning from work, including personal, professional, and health-related problems.

marginal - (adj.) very small or minimal in amount; nearly unacceptable in performance. e.g. - The company will have to close down if its profits continue to be only marginal. Der. (n.) margin; (adv.) marginally.

materialize - (v.) to appear or come into existence or reality. e.g. - Her dream of becoming a dancer failed to materialize when she was paralyzed in the accident. Der. (n.) materialization.

menace - (n.) threat or danger. e.g. - Drugs and guns are a menace to the well-being of today's youth. Der. (v.) menace; (adj.) menacing; (adv.) menacingly.

mettle - (n.) strength of character; courage. e.g. - The paramedic displayed great mettle in rescuing the man from the burning car.

migrate - (v.) to leave one climate for another for the purpose of breeding or feeding. e.g. - Geese migrate south during the winter in order to find food in a warmer climate. Der. (n.) migration; (adj.) migrating.

militia - (n.) a group of individuals organized for the purpose of military service. e.g. - The militia carried out many exercises in order to prepare for war.

mischievous - (adj.) causing trouble or annoyance. e.g. - The teacher sent the mischievous pupil to the principal's office. Der. (n.) mischief; (adv.) mischievously.

misconstrue - (v.) to misunderstand. e.g. - You have completely misconstrued what I said. When I said you looked beautiful today, I didn't mean that you usually look ugly. Der. (adj.) misconstruable.

misgiving - (n.) doubt; uncertainty. e.g. - She had misgivings about marrying him when she discovered that he had a prison record.

mitigate - (v.) to lessen the severity of; (syn.) extenuate. e.g. - Your apology does not mitigate the seriousness of your mistake. Der. (n.) mitigation; (adj.) mitigating; (adj.) mitigated (ant.) unmitigated.

momentous - (adj.) notable; significant; important. e.g. - Her wedding day was one of the most momentous events of her life.

monetary - (adj.) relating to money, finance, or the economy. e.g. - The study of economics involves many monetary theories.

morsel - (n.) a small portion of food. e.g. - A morsel of food is not going to satisfy his appetite.

mouth off - (id.) to be rude or impudent. e.g. - You should be punished for mouthing off to your parents.

munch - (v.) to make a noise from the mouth while eating. e.g. - I hate the way you munch your food. Can't you eat more quietly?

municipal - (adj.) relating to the city. e.g. - The municipal authorities pay for the upkeep of city property. Der. (n.) municipality.

murky - (adj.) dark; unclear. e.g. - The water in the lake was murky. The bottom of the lake could not be seen. Der. (n.) murk, murkiness; (adv.) murkily.

neutral - (adj.) lacking in color. e.g. - Their living room has a neutral color scheme and is predominantly beige and white. Der. (adv.) neutrally.

nibble - (v.) to eat with very small bites. e.g. - By the way you are nibbling at your food, I take it that you're not very hungry. Der. (n.) nibble.

nitpick - (id.) to be overly concerned with very small details. e.g. - My boss is very demanding and nit-picks the smallest details.

nitwit - (id.) an idiot; a stupid person. e.g. - If you don't know that two and two equals four, you are a bigger nitwit than I thought.

no "if's", "and's" or "but's" - (id.) no excuses will be accepted. e.g. - You will do your homework. No "if's", "and's" or "but's"!

nominate - (v.) to select a candidate for a particular duty, esp. for public office. e.g. - The class nominated Abdul as their class president in the school election. Der. (n.) nomination.

notion - idea, theory, or belief. e.g. - Where did you get the crazy notion that the moon is made of cheese?

notorious - (adj.) relating to fame for despicable or blameworthy events or crimes. e.g. - He is notorious for having committed bank robbery, so everyone recognizes him. Der. (n.) notoriety; (adv.) notoriously.

noxious - (adj.) the quality of possessing a poisonous or deadly gas. e.g. - Gasoline is a noxious substance. Breathing excessive quantities of it can cause death. Der. (n.) noxiousness; (adv.) noxiously.

obliterate - (v.) to wipe out or destroy. e.g. - Many people fear that the world may be obliterated by nuclear war. Der. (n.) obliteration.

obsequious - (adj.) behaving like a servant; servile; obedient. e.g. - The waitress was obsequious towards the demanding customer and brought him whatever he asked for. Der. (adv.) obsequiously.

obsession - (n.) a continuing mental preoccupation with a single thought or idea which is often unreasonable or illogical. e.g. - He continued his obsession with finding a cure for his disease long after the doctor had told him that treatment was impossible. Der. (adj.) obsessive.

obsolete - (adj.) relating to things which are no longer useful as a result of being replaced or becoming outdated. e.g. - Computers become obsolete quickly nowadays as they are constantly being replaced by newer models. Der. (n.) obsolescence.

obstacle - (n.) something which holds back, delays, or prevents progress; impediment; (syn.) hindrance, stumbling block, barrier. e.g. - Despite the obstacle of being deaf, Beethoven was able to compose his final symphonies.

obstinacy - (n.) the action of being rigid in opinion; stubbornness. e.g. - He has displayed great obstinacy on this subject. I don't think that he's going to change his mind. Der. (adj.) obstinate; (adv.) obstinately.

odious - (adj.) deserving of hate; (syn.) despicable. e.g. - He was convicted of the odious crime of murdering small children.

on schedule - (id.) to be on time. e.g. - The bus is on schedule today. We should get to work on time.

once in a blue moon - (id.) something that happens very rarely. e.g. - I don't like bowling, so I do it only once in a blue moon.

opponent - (n.) enemy; antagonist; (syn.) adversary. e.g. - They are hardly friends. In fact, they are bitter opponents.

orchard - (n.) a group of fruit, nut, or olive trees; (syn.) grove. e.g. - The farm has an orchard containing apple and pear trees.

ordeal - (n.) a difficult or trying experience. e.g. - Cancer patients undergoing chemotherapy must endure a difficult ordeal.

ornate - (adj.) heavily or ostentatiously decorated. e.g. - The ornate castle was decorated with gold and silver, as well as priceless rugs and paintings. Der. (n.) ornateness; (adv.) ornately.

ostensibly - (adv.) in appearance. e.g. - Ostensibly John is a nice guy, but when you get to know him, you realize that he isn't. Der. (adj.) ostensible.

ostentatious - (adj.) relating to an obvious display, esp. of wealth. e.g. - It was very ostentatious of Elizabeth to wear such expensive jewelry to a charity event. Der. (adv.) ostentatiously.

out of the question - (id.) something that is impossible even to consider. e.g. - Going on vacation this year is out of the question. We just don't have enough money.

ovation - (n.) applause. e.g. - The singer received a standing ovation after his performance. Nothing could be heard over the sound of the applause.

overabundance - (n.) a huge or plentiful amount. e.g. - An overabundance of rain can result in flooding.

overstay one's welcome - (id.) to stay longer than one is welcome; to begin to impose upon one's host. e.g. - It was obvious that we had overstayed our welcome when she asked us if we would leave her house as soon as possible.

overtone - (n.) suggestion or implication; hidden meaning. e.g. - I don't like what you are implying. The overtone is that I'm fat and stupid.

overwhelm - (v.) to overcome or take control of an individual's thoughts, feelings, or actions. e.g. - He was overwhelmed with sadness when his wife died.

Exercises – M to O

Instructions: Complete the sentences below, using one of the words beginning with the letters "M" to "O" from the previous section. Note that some gaps require a single word, while others may need a phrasal verb or idiomatic expression. You may also need to change the form of the word. The answers are provided at the end of book.

1) The houses in that town were _____ by the tornado.

2) The political party _____ their candidate in the election.

3) She is so _____. I have never met anyone so stubborn.

4) He got fat due to eating an _____ of food.

5) She complains and _____ about the smallest and most insignificant things.

6) The large amount of donations given to charity during times of natural disaster shows the _____ of the general public.

7) Those chemicals are _____. You can die if you consume even small quantities of them.

8) Taking the foundation course is _____. Every student has to take it.

9) His tastes are very _____, and he likes to show off his wealth.

10) The mother's grief and rage about the murder of her daughter _____ her attack on the killer.

Words – P

Instructions: Study the words below, paying attention to their meanings as well as how they are used in the example sentences. Then complete the exercise that follows.

paramount - (adj.) highly important or significant. e.g. - If you want to get good grades, studying is paramount.

parsimonious - (adj.) exhibiting excessive or extreme care about money and spending. e.g. - The parsimonious man used his tea bags twice in order to save money. Der. (n.) parsimony; (adv.) parsimoniously.

partake - (v.) to take part in an activity with others; to participate. e.g. - Suki could not partake in the basketball game because she had just broken her leg.

patent - (adj.) obvious; not hidden; visible. e.g. - The television had a patent defect. The crack in the screen was clearly visible. Der. (adv.) patently; (ant.) latent.

patriotism - (n.) the love for or loyalty to an individual's country of nationality or citizenship. e.g. - Feelings of patriotism are high on Independence Day. Der. (n.) patriot.

patronize - (v.) to act as a regular customer; to provide economic support. e.g. - He regularly patronizes the restaurant on the corner. He eats there five times a week.

peak - (n.) the highest point. e.g. - There is a great view of the city from the peak of that mountain. Der. (v.) peak; (adj.) peaked.

peculiar - (adj.) strange; weird. e.g. - Rosa looked really peculiar in her strange clothes and heavy make-up. Der. (n.) peculiarity; (adv.) peculiarly.

peeling - (n.) the skin of a fruit or vegetable. e.g. - The peeling of a banana must be removed before it can be eaten. Der. (v.) peel.

penchant - (n.) desire or preference. e.g. - Cheng is reckless and has a penchant for participating in dangerous activities.

penetrate - (v.) to enter inside, esp. with force. e.g. - The police penetrated the house where the criminals were hiding by breaking down the front door. Der. (n.) penetration; (adj.) penetrative, penetrable; penetrating; (adv.) penetratingly.

penitence - (n.) the feeling of deep regret or sorrow about one's wrongdoings; (syn.) remorse, contrition. e.g. - The murderer feels deep penitence for his crimes and made a full public apology to the victims' families. Der. (adj.) penitential.

perceptible - (adj.) capable of being understood by the senses. e.g. - There has been a very perceptible change in Nadira's behavior. She used to be quite shy, but now is outspoken. Der. (n.) perception; (v.) perceive; (adv.) perceptibly.

perfidy - (n.) disloyalty or treason toward an individual's country of national origin. e.g. - The American, Benedict Arnold, was guilty of perfidy when he told U.S. military secrets to the British during the American Revolutionary War.

perjury - (n.) the action of lying while giving a sworn statement in court. e.g. - The witness committed perjury by saying that the suspect was with her at the time of the crime, although he was not. Der. (v.) perjure.

perpetually - (adv.) continuously. e.g. - I have never seen anyone as talkative as her. She talks perpetually. Der. (n.) perpetuation; (v.) perpetuate; (adj.) perpetual.

perturb - (v.) to cause disorder or annoyance. e.g. - The little girl's tantrum greatly perturbed her mother. Der. (n.) perturbation; (adj.) perturbable.

peruse - (v.) to read sthg, esp. carefully or for specific information. e.g. - Hasin perused the book before deciding it was interesting enough to buy. Der. (n.) perusal.

pervasive - (adj.) affecting all parts of something. e.g.- The changes to the system are pervasive; therefore, the system will need to be completely redone. Der. (n.) pervasion, pervasiveness; (v.) pervade; (adv.) pervasively.

pessimism - (n.) behavior marked by expecting the worst to happen. e.g. - Deven has had a lot of bad luck in his life so, understandably, he views his future with pessimism. Der. (adj.) pessimistic; (adv.) pessimistically.

phlegmatic - (adj.) calm and unemotional. e.g. - He is so phlegmatic. I've never seen him get nervous under pressure. Der. (adv.) phlegmatically.

phony - (adj.) false, artificial, or insincere. e.g. - Her apology was phony. You should have known that she was being insincere.

pick a fight - (id.) to encourage a physical attack by displaying a hostile attitude. e.g. - He picked a fight by saying that I was too weak to hit him.

picked over - (id.) being of limited variety because other individuals have already chosen the best items. e.g. - The fruit at the grocery store was picked over because we arrived too late in the day.

pillage - (n.) the action of robbing or seizing objects, such as in a war. e.g. - The pillage of many stores occurred during the Los Angeles riots when much valuable merchandise was stolen. Der. (v.) pillage.

pin your hopes on sthg - (id.) to be very hopeful that something will happen. e.g. - I wouldn't <u>pin you hopes on</u> being accepted into medical school. You know how tough the competition is.

pinch pennies - (id.) to be very economical with money or in spending. e.g. - He is <u>pinching pennies</u> because he lost his job last month.

pioneer - (n.) an individual who goes into unexplored territory. e.g. - The <u>pioneers</u> traveled west to unsettled land. Der. (v.) pioneer; (adj.) pioneering.

pique - (v.) to irritate or provoke. e.g. - You <u>piqued</u> my curiosity by telling me that you have a surprise for me. Please tell me more.

pittance - (n.) a very small wage or amount of money. e.g. - Kazuo makes such a <u>pittance</u> at work that he can hardly feed his children.

play with fire - (id.) to become involved in a dangerous situation. e.g. - If you decide to cheat on the test, you're really <u>playing with fire</u>.

plentiful - (adj.) abundant; more than enough. e.g. - Plants cannot grow without <u>plentiful</u> sunshine. Der. (n.) plenty; (adv.) plentifully.

plot - (n.) the organization or plan of a story. e.g. - The <u>plot</u> of the story was about two twins who had been separated at birth. Der. (v.) plot.

plump - (adj.) fat; thick and round. e.g. - <u>Plump</u> tomatoes make better spaghetti sauce. Smaller ones aren't usually as tasty. Der. (v.) plumpen.

ponder - (v.) to think about or consider deeply. e.g. - He sat by the lake for hours <u>pondering</u> the meaning of life. Der. (adj.) ponderable.

populace - (n.) people residing in a certain area. e.g. - The <u>populace</u> of the city of Chicago is asked to limit its electricity use during the summer. Der. (n.) population; (v.) populate; (adj.) populated.

posterity - (n.) future generations; descendants. e.g. - The rich man invested his money wisely so that his <u>posterity</u> would have a large inheritance.

potential - (adj.) possible; capable of becoming fact. e.g. - Every job applicant is considered to be a <u>potential</u> employee. Der. (n.) potential; (adv.) potentially.

precarious - (adj.) dangerous; (syn.) treacherous. e.g. - His car was hanging off the side of the mountain in a <u>precarious</u> position after the accident. Der. (n.) precariousness; (adv.) precariously.

precedent - (n.) a previous event, esp. one which establishes a pattern for subsequent behavior. e.g. - The judge sentenced the criminal to the death penalty. This set a precedent for the use of the death penalty for subsequent crimes. Der. (v.) precede.

precinct - (n.) territory of a city established for police control. e.g. - New York City has many police precincts, which are usually established according to neighborhood boundaries.

precipitate - (v.) to cause or bring about, especially suddenly. e.g. - The violence precipitated full-scale war. Der. (n.) precipitation; (adj.) precipitous.

predator - (n.) an individual or animal that preys or kills. e.g. - The American black bear is a predator because it kills other animals and sometimes humans.

predicament - (n.) dilemma; difficult situation. e.g. - He was left in a predicament when his car broke down on the freeway at 4:00 a.m.

predilection - (n.) a desire or preference. e.g. - She has an overwhelming predilection for chocolate and always wants to eat it.

predominant - (adj.) playing a major or significant role; (syn.) prominent. e.g. - He was a predominant contributor to the hospital building fund, donating over $1,000,000. Der. (n.) predomination; (v.) predominate; (adv.) predominantly.

prematurely - (adv.) too early. e.g. - The baby was born prematurely in March. It shouldn't have been born until May. Der. (adj.) premature.

premise - (n.) an area of land which contains buildings. e.g. - Rashid is a security guard at the factory. His job is to protect the premises against theft.

prerogative - (n.) a special option, decision, or privilege. e.g. - She wasn't required to attend the lesson. On the contrary, it was her prerogative.

prevalent - (adj.) commonly practiced; continuing in use or acceptance; (syn.) widespread. e.g. - Skiing is prevalent in mountainous areas. Der. (v.) prevail; (adj.) prevalently.

pricey - (id.) very expensive. e.g. - They can eat at that pricey restaurant because they have a lot of money.

proliferation - (n.) an amount which is excessive in growth or quantity; plethora. e.g. - J.S. Bach composed a proliferation of symphonies in his lifetime. Der. (v.) proliferate; (adj.) prolific: (adv.) prolifically.

prominent - (adj.) playing a major or significant role. e.g. - Your grades in high school play a prominent role in determining which college you can attend. Der. (n.) prominence; (adv.) prominently.

prompt - (v.) to cause; to bring about a result or action. e.g. - The rainy weather prompted the cancellation of the baseball game.

prone (to) - (adj.) having a certain tendency or vulnerability. e.g. - Nico is clumsy and is therefore prone to accidents. Der. (n.) proneness; (adv.) pronely.

propensity - (n) a desire or preference that appears natural to a certain person. e.g. - His propensity to overeat is obvious because he is so overweight. Der. (v.) propend; (adj.) propense.

proposition - (n.) a problem put forward for consideration. e.g. - The city considered the mayor's proposition to build a new road through the city center. Der. (v.) propose.

prosecute - (v.) to take to court for the commission of a crime. e.g. - The suspect was prosecuted in court for murder and was found not guilty. Der. (n.) prosecution.

prostrate - (adj.) lying in a face-down position; sometimes used to describe an act of worship. e.g. - The patient was lying prostrate after his heart attack and had to be turned face-up so that first aid could be administered.

protocol - (n.) standards of conduct. e.g. - Old-fashioned protocol dictated that men should always open doors for women.

protract - (v.) to continue for an extended time. e.g. - The journey was protracted by several delays as a result of the bad weather conditions.

provident - (adj.) the provision for unforeseen events in the future; careful; prudent. e.g. - It was very provident of you to bring an umbrella as rain is forecast. Der. (n.) providence.

provoke - (v.) to cause or incite anger. e.g. - Her outrageous behavior provoked her father and caused him to scream and yell at her. Der. (n.) provocation; (adj.) provocative; (adv.) provocatively.

prudence - (n.) the exercise of care or caution. e.g. - You must exercise prudence in your investments. Otherwise, you might lose a substantial amount of money. Der. (adj.) prudent; (adv.) prudently; (ant.) imprudent.

pugnacious - (adj.) exceptionally aggressive or quarrelsome in behavior. e.g. - Sean is so pugnacious. He is always trying to start arguments. Der. (adv.) pugnaciously.

pull through - (id.) to survive an accident or illness. e.g. - The doctors say that Kareem will pull through his accident.

punch - (v.) to hit with a closed hand. e.g. - The boxer fell to the floor when he was punched by his opponent. Der. (n.) punch.

purge - (v.) to dispose of, esp. with force. e.g. - The hospital attendants had to pump the child's stomach in order to purge the poison from his body. Der. (n.) purge.

pursuit - (n.) a hobby or undertaking. e.g. - His favorite pursuits include stamp collecting and playing the guitar. Der. (v.) pursue.

put yourself in my shoes - (id.) to try to understand the situation another person is in. e.g. - If you'd put yourself in my shoes, you would understand why I did what I had to do.

putrid - (adj.) being highly unpleasant or repugnant; rotten. e.g. - This food is putrid and is not fit to eat. Der. (adv.) putridly.

Exercises – P

Instructions: Complete the sentences below, using one of the words beginning with the letter "P" from the previous section. Note that some gaps require a single word, while others may need a phrasal verb or idiomatic expression. You may also need to change the form of the word. The answers are provided at the end of book.

1) She was very _____ when she spoke to the group. She didn't appear nervous at all.

2) Small villages were often _____ in the Middle Ages as attackers and raiders stole the possessions of the local people.

3) The _____ of the mountain is 12,000 feet above sea level.

4) He was a _____ in the field of bio-engineering. In fact, he was the first scientist to devote himself to research in the area.

5) The child was lying in a _____ position after the accident.

6) That cheese is _____. You will get sick if you eat it.

7) She is _____ if she is thinking about lying to her parents.

8) The completion of the project was _____ by several months because of a lack of financing.

9) There has been a _____ shift in the attitude of the class after the teacher told us off. Some students used to disrespect the teacher, but they don't anymore.

10) The specialist said she would _____ her cancer treatment and make a full recovery.

Words – Q to R

Instructions: Study the words below, paying attention to their meanings as well as how they are used in the example sentences. Then complete the exercise that follows.

quaint - (adj.) charming and old-fashioned. e.g. - The old-fashioned Austrian village had a quaint atmosphere.

quarters - (n.) accommodation, usually for soldiers or animals. e.g. - Soldiers on the army base sleep in shared quarters containing twelve beds.

quarry - (n.) an open area from which rock, such as marble, is removed. e.g. - The workers were removing rock and marble from the quarry, using heavy machinery.

querulous - (adj.) characterized by constant complaining. e.g. - The man became querulous in old age and began to complain about everything. Der. (n.) querulousness; (adv.) querulously.

quest - (n.) a mission or adventure in pursuit of a specific purpose. e.g. - The doctors went on a quest to the African jungle to find rare plants to use in the manufacture of medicine.

quirk - (n.) unnatural behavior or affectation; idiosyncrasy. e.g. - Jodi has the strange quirk of checking her alarm clock ten times before going to bed. Der. (n.) quirkiness; (adj.) quirky; (adv.) quirkily.

racy - (adj.) sexually suggestive or sensational. e.g. - The actress wore a racy dress which was very low-cut in the front.

radical - (adj.) extreme; non-conservative; non-traditional. e.g. - He has radical political theories. In fact, he believes that the government should be abolished entirely. Der. (adv.) radically.

rancid - (adj.) having a bad smell or taste. e.g. - You had better not eat that food. It is rancid. Der. (n.) rancidity, rancidness; (adv.) rancidly.

ransack - (v.) to throw into disorder or disorganization as a result of searching for valuables, esp. during a burglary. e.g. - The burglars ransacked the house in search of jewelry and money. Der. (adj.) ransacked.

ransom - (1)(n.) the rescue from captivity by paying money; (2)(met.) release from punishment. e.g. - (1) The kidnapping victim was released after the ransom was paid. (2) Many religions believe in ransom for the punishment for sins.

rapt - (adj.) totally attracted to; (syn.) enchanted. e.g. - The children were giving their rapt attention to the TV program and didn't hear their mother calling them to dinner. Der. (v.) enrapture.

ravine - (n.) a small valley with steep sides. e.g. - A ravine had been formed in the field where a small fresh-water spring used to flow.

reap - (v.)(met.) to win, acquire, or attain. e.g. - After years of hard work, he finally reaped some benefit from his efforts.

receptacle - (n.) a container used for collecting items which are later thrown away. e.g. - All litter should be thrown into the receptacles provided throughout the park.

recess - (v.) to interrupt or suspend an activity or procedure. e.g. - The children are not in class right now. They have recessed for lunch. Der. (n.) recess.

recession - (1)(n.) a group which leaves at the end of a ceremony; (2)(n.) a decline in the general economy. e.g. - (1) It took the funeral recession half an hour to cross the road since thousands of people had attended. (2) Jobs are difficult to find during an economic recession. Der. (v.) recede.

recite - (v.) to say or repeat a script from memory. e.g. - All students will be expected to memorize "The Gettysburg Address" and recite it to the class before the end of the term. Der. (n.) recital, recitation; (adj.) recited.

recover with flying colors - (id.) to recover very well after an accident or injury. e.g. - Husna is recovering with flying colors after her operation and should be out of the hospital by the weekend.

recruitment - (n.) the process of adding new individuals to activities of employment. e.g. - He works for an employment agency. His job is the recruitment of new managers for employment with various companies. Der. (v.) recruit.

rectify - (v.) to make right or correct. e.g. - The bank has promised to rectify the error they made on my account. Der. (n.) rectification; (adj.) rectified.

recuperate - (v.) to recover health after an extended illness or operation; (syn.) convalesce. e.g. - He is in bed recuperating after suffering another heart attack. Der. (n.) recuperation.

red tape - (id.) complications or paperwork involved in government procedures or bureaucracy. e.g. - Applying for a job with the government involves a lot of red tape.

refectory - (n.) a place for eating and drinking. e.g. - The students were gathered in the refectory, eating their lunch.

refinement - (n.) the action of improving or perfecting. e.g. - Petroleum oil must go through refinement before it can be used as gasoline. Der. (v.) refine; (adj.) refined.

refrain (from) - (v.) to restrain or prevent oneself from doing something. e.g. - The hospital is a smoke-free zone. That means you must refrain from smoking.

regime - (n.) a strict form of management or government. e.g. - Fang has a strict exercise regime. She goes to the gym every day.

register - (v.) to officially record an individual's name in a book or list. e.g. - Daksha registered for classes at California State University last week. Der. (n.) registration.

regress - (v.) to return to an earlier time period. e.g. - Being overwhelmed by the responsibilities of adult life, Haru wished that she could regress to her childhood. Der. (n.) regression.

rehabilitation - (n.) the action of returning to a state of good health, esp. through the use of therapy. e.g. - After years of alcoholism, Lindsay is finally undergoing rehabilitation in order to stop drinking. Der. (v.) rehabilitate; (adj.) rehabilitated.

rehearsal - (n.) a preparatory performance or recital. e.g. - The orchestra had several rehearsals before they held a concert for the public. Der. (v.) rehearse; (adj.) rehearsed.

reiterate - (v.) to repeat or emphasize again. e.g. - The teacher reiterated the instructions to the examination after the student asked a question about them. Der. (n.) reiteration; (adj.) reiterative; (adv.) reiteratively.

relapse - (n.) the action of returning to a previous condition, esp. for the worse; deterioration. e.g. - Kendra had not used drugs for years, but she had a relapse last weekend. Der. (v.) relapse.

relegate - (v.) to assign to an inferior group or category. e.g. - The baseball player was relegated to the minor league when he began to play poorly. Der. (n.) relegation.

relic - (n.) an item of historical or archeological significance. e.g. - The Museum of Natural History contains many archeological relics, many of which are over 2,000 years old.

relinquish - (v.) to surrender or give up. e.g. - The single mother was forced to relinquish her children to the state when she was sentenced to prison. Der. (n.) relinquishment.

relish - (v.) to enjoy very much. e.g. - I relish long walks in the open air during the summer.

reluctant - (adj.) hesitant or unready to act. e.g. - Deepal was reluctant to accept the job when she heard that the salary was quite low. Der. (n.) reluctance; (adv.) reluctantly.

remedy - (n.) a cure or therapy. e.g. - A common remedy for headache is aspirin. Der. (v.) remedy; (adj.) remedial.

remorse - (n.) the feeling of guilt or sadness about one's own wrongdoings; (syn.) penitence, contrition. e.g. - The murderer showed great remorse for his crimes and asked for the forgiveness of the public. Der. (adj.) remorseful; (adv.) remorsefully.

remunerate - (v.) to pay for a service performed; compensate. e.g. - The company agreed to remunerate me quite highly. My salary will be $20,000 a month. Der. (n.) remuneration; (adj.) remunerated.

render - (v.) to give or provide, esp. a service. e.g. - You must pay the applicable fee for any services rendered to you.

renounce - (v.) to refuse to obey or recognize the authority of. e.g. - Many people who renounced Hitler during World War II were put to death. Der. (n.) renouncement.

renovate - (v.) to renew; to improve the condition of. e.g. - That hotel is currently being renovated. They are repairing the damage caused by the fire. Der. (n.) renovation; (adj.) renovated.

repel - (v.) to push back or away. e.g. - This spray repels mosquitoes because the smell is offensive to them. Der. (n.) repulsion, repellent; (adj.) repulsive.

repent - (v.) to ask forgiveness for a sin or wrongdoing. e.g. - I forgave her after she sincerely repented and apologized. Der. (n.) repentance.

replete (with) - (adj.) complete; abundant. e.g. - The orchestra was replete with all types of wind and string instruments. Der. (n.) repleteness, repletion.

reprehensible - (adj.) suitable of receiving great blame or criticism; (syn.) culpable. e.g. - Committing murder is a reprehensible act. Der. (n.) reprehension, reprehensibility; (v.) reprehend; (adv.) reprehensibly.

reproach - (v.) to give severe criticism or blame. e.g. - The mother reproached her child for spilling the milk. Der. (n.) reproach; (adj.) reproachful; (adv.) reproachfully; (exp.) beyond reproach.

reproduce - (v.) to prepare a copy of something from its original source. e.g. - The secretary reproduced the contract by making a photocopy. Der. (n.) reproduction; (adj.) reproduced.

residue - (n.) part of something which is left over after the main part has been taken away. e.g. - I hate this soap. It leaves a strange residue on my skin that can't be rinsed off. Der. (adj.) residual; (adv.) residually.

resign yourself to a situation - (id.) to accept a bad situation and stop attempting to change it for the better. e.g. - Bettina used to hate living with her mother-in-law, but has finally resigned herself to the situation.

resolute - (adj.) acting decisively and with determination. e.g. - He was resolute in his decision to attend college. In fact, he said that nothing could change his mind. Der. (n.) resolve; (v.) resolve; (adv.) resolutely.

respiration - (n.) the action of breathing. e.g. - Respiration and heart beat must be present in order for an individual to remain alive after an accident. Der. (v.) respire.

reticent - (adj.) reluctant or unwilling to talk. e.g. - The suspect was reticent when asked about his participation in the crime.

retire - (v.) to go to bed. e.g. - I feel tired and would like to retire for the evening.

retract - (v.) to draw back; to withdraw. e.g. - The newspaper retracted the false information that it gave in the article and offered a full apology.

retreat - (n.) a private place, often used to spend time alone. e.g. - Kiku's husband is away for the weekend on a retreat in the mountains. Der. (v.) retreat.

retrieve - (v.) to get or bring back again. e.g. - The information could not be retrieved from the computer system. It must not have been stored properly in the memory. Der. (n.) retrieval; (adj.) retrievable.

retrospect - (n.) the examination of an event after it has occurred. e.g. - In retrospect, he realizes that it was a mistake to have taken the job. Der. (adj.) retrospective; (adv.) retrospectively.

revel - (v.) to celebrate, esp. wildly. e.g. - They reveled all night at the party and were still drunk in the morning. Der. (n.) revelry.

revile - (v.) to criticize severely; scold; chide; rebuke; (syn.) reproach. e.g. - The newspaper article reviled the government for not providing adequate funding for educational programs.

ring a bell - (id.) to sound familiar. e.g. - Now that you mention it, that story does ring a bell.

ringleader - (n.) leader of a group that participates in illegal activities. e.g. - The ringleader of the gang is thought to have organized the sale of narcotic drugs.

rivalry - (n.) competition; opposition. e.g. - The two opposing basketball teams engage in a friendly rivalry. Der. (n.) rival; (v.) rival.

rodent - (n.) a small unwanted animal, such as a rat or a mouse. e.g. - You can set a trap or use poison to deal with rodents in your home.

roomy - (adj.) having enough space or room; (syn.) spacious. e.g. - The hotel was quite roomy and could accommodate 2,000 guests. Der. (n.) roominess.

rudimentary - (adj.) basic or fundamental. e.g. - You will never understand advanced mathematics if you don't learn the rudimentary principles of arithmetic. Der. (n.) rudiment; (adv.) rudimentarily.

rummage - (v.) to cause disorder while searching for something. e.g. - We rummaged through the attic looking for old photographs. Der. (adj.) rummage.

ruthless - (adj.) cruel; malicious. e.g. - He is known for especially ruthless crimes against the elderly. Der. (n.) ruthlessness; (adv.) ruthlessly.

Exercises – Q to R

Instructions: Complete the sentences below, using one of the words beginning with the letters "Q" or "R" from the previous section. Note that some gaps require a single word, while others may need a phrasal verb or idiomatic expression. You may also need to change the form of the word. The answers are provided at the end of book.

1) After years of drug addiction, she is finally undergoing _____.

2) The company will begin to _____ the service once you have paid the deposit.

3) The _____ restaurant tried to recreate the atmosphere of the 1950s.

4) You will need a few months to _____ after your back operation is done.

5) The explorer went on a _____ to India to try to find the endangered species of tigers.

6) The president had to _____ control of the company after the merger was complete.

7) The army officer's job is the _____ of new soldiers.

8) Her _____ of constantly pushing her glasses up her nose gets a bit distracting.

9) In _____, he wishes that he had gone to college after all.

10) I was _____ to lie to the police officer since I knew the punishment would be severe.

Words – S

Instructions: Study the words below, paying attention to their meanings as well as how they are used in the example sentences. Then complete the exercise that follows.

sacred - (adj.) reverent; holy; (syn.) pious. e.g. – Temples, mosques, and churches are considered sacred since religious worship occurs there.

sag - (v.) to lose tightness or firmness. e.g. - She doesn't look young anymore. Her skin has started to sag and wrinkle. Der. (n.) (adj.) sagging; (adj.) sagged.

salvage - (v.) to save something, esp. that which has been damaged. e.g. - It was possible to salvage the car after the accident. It is being fixed at the garage right now. Der. (n.) salvage; (adj.) salvageable.

sanctimonious - (adj.) relating to an insincere or hypocritical adherence to high moral standards. e.g. - The wealthy king gave a sanctimonious speech about how money should not be considered the most important thing in life. Der. (n.) sanctimony, sanctimoniousness; (adv.) sanctimoniously.

saunter - (v.) to walk in an unhurried manner; (syn.) stroll. e.g. - The couple slowly sauntered down the street, looking in the store windows. Der. (n.) saunter.

scald - (v.) to burn with hot water. e.g. - The hot coffee spilled, scalding the baby's skin and causing it to turn red. Der. (adj.) scalding, scalded.

scant - (adj.) a very small amount. Due to scant attendance, class was cancelled. Der. (adj.) scanty; (adv.) scantily.

scarlet - (adj.) bright red. e.g. - Her face turned scarlet from being in the sun too long.

scathing - (adj.) harsh; severe; damaging. e.g. - The senator presented a scathing attack on the proposed law. Der. (n.) scathe; (v.) scathe; (adv.) scathingly.

scorch - (v.) to burn with dry heat. e.g. - He scorched the shirt while ironing it, leaving a huge burn on the sleeve. Der. (adj.) scorched.

scrape - (n.) an area on the body where the surface of the skin has been removed. e.g. - The child fell off his bicycle and got a scrape on his knee from the rough pavement. Der. (v.) scrape; (adj.) scraped.

scribbled - (adj.) written in an illegible or disorganized manner. e.g. - Can you make out this scribbled message? The handwriting is so unclear that I can't read it. Der. (n.) scribble; (v.) scribble.

script - (n.) a written, detailed plan, such as for a play or movie. e.g. - The actor studied the script in order to memorize his part.

scrumptious - (adj.) delicious; very tasty; (syn.) delectable. e.g. - This cake is scrumptious. I have never tasted anything so delicious.

scruples - (n.) morals; ethics; standards of behavior. e.g. - People displaying immoral behavior do not have the proper scruples. Der. (adj.) scrupulous; (adv.) scrupulously; (ant.) unscrupulous.

scrutinize - (v.) to examine in great detail. e.g. - He scrutinized the artwork in order to determine if it was authentic. Der. (n.) scrutiny.

seal - (n.) a stamp or symbol. e.g. - Your diploma contains the official college seal in the lower left-hand corner.

search high and low - (id.) to search for something extensively. e.g. - I've searched high and low for my car keys, but I still can't find them.

secession - (n.) the action of taking back membership or property from a group or union; withdrawal. e.g. - The secession of a small group of citizens reduced the town's population. Der. (v.) secede.

sect - (n.) a group observing certain religious beliefs which are often strict or fanatical. e.g. - Certain religious sects require their followers to have short hair and wear only simple clothing.

sedate - (v.) to make calm or quiet, esp. with the use of medication. e.g. - The doctor sedated the patient with tranquilizers. Der. (n.) sedation; (adj.) sedate; (adj.) sedated.

seize - (v.) to take hold of something with force or strength. e.g. - The policeman seized the escaped criminal by grabbing him with both arms. Der. (n.) seizure.

sentence (to) - (v.) to specify the punishment for a criminal convicted of a crime. e.g. - The attacker was sentenced to seven years in prison for his involvement in the assault on the elderly woman. Der. (n.) sentence.

sentry - (n.) a soldier standing guard. e.g. - A sentry was standing guard at the main gate of the army base.

sequence - (n.) the order or series of individual items. e.g. - The files should be organized in numerical sequence from one to one hundred. Der. (v.) sequence; (adj.) sequential; (adv.) sequentially.

serene - (adj.) peaceful; (syn.) placid. e.g. - They enjoyed serene surroundings during their vacation at an isolated cabin in the north woods. Der. (n.) serenity; (adv.) serenely.

servility - (n.) relating to the behavior of a servant or an individual in an inferior position. e.g. - The employee responded with complete servility, doing whatever his boss demanded. Der. (adj.) servile; (adv.) servilely.

set sbdy straight - (id.) to point out a mistake in another person's behavior or thinking. e.g. - I need to set you straight. The bus leaves at 3:00, not 3:30.

set the record straight - (id.) to provide someone with correct information after they have been misinformed. e.g. - I want to set the record straight. I paid $2 for the tickets, not $20.

setback - (n.) an event which causes a reversal in progress. e.g. - The poor weather conditions caused a setback to our journey, and we were delayed three hours. Der. (ph. v.) set back.

severity - (n.) seriousness. e.g. - The severity of punishment shall be equal to the seriousness of the crime. Der. (adj.) severe; (adv.) severely.

shady - (adj.) being of doubtful quality or character; dubious. e.g. - Maybe people do change, but I think he's a shady character.

shed light on sthg - (id.) to explain. e.g. - Could you shed some light on this homework?

shell - (v.) to drop bombs. e.g. - When London was heavily shelled during World War II, its residents often took shelter in subway tunnels to avoid being killed in the bombing. Der. (n.) shell.

shelter - (n.) something that provides cover and protection. e.g. - We took shelter under a tree when it started to rain. Der. (v.) shelter; (adj.) sheltered.

show sbdy the ropes - (id.) to provide someone with instructions. e.g. - He showed me the ropes on my first day of work.

skeletons in your closet - (id.) to hide secrets about your past. e.g. - Nina doesn't talk a lot about her past. I wonder if she has skeletons in her closet.

shred - (v.) to cut or tear into small pieces. e.g. - Cheese is usually shredded before it is placed on the top of pizza. Der. (n.) shredder; (adj.) shredded.

shrewd - (adj.) possessing awareness and cleverness in business dealings. e.g. - He is a very shrewd businessperson and now owns over 200 convenience stores. Der. (n.) shrewdness; (adv.) shrewdly.

shrill - (adj.) sharp; high pitched. e.g. - Your voice is very shrill. I think you are singing in the wrong key.

shrivel - (v.) to cause to become wrinkled from age or lack of moisture. My grandmother's skin shriveled as she became older. Der. (adj.) shriveled.

shrug - (v.) to move the shoulders upwards to show disinterest or uncertainty. e.g. - When I asked Whitney if she would go to the party, she just shrugged her shoulders and changed the subject.

simmer - (v.) to cook over a low heat. e.g. - This soup should be simmered for thirty minutes at a low temperature.

simulate - (v.) to reproduce or copy the appearance of. e.g. - The restaurant tries to simulate the atmosphere from the 1950's. Der. (n.) simulation; (adj.) simulated.

simultaneously - (adv.) at the same time. e.g. - Twins or triplets celebrate their birthdays simultaneously. Der. (n.) simultaneousness, simultaneity; (adj.) simultaneous.

sinecure - (n.) employment for which an individual is paid, but for which no duties or responsibilities are required. e.g. - Haaziq is retired now. His job as city clerk is only a sinecure since he doesn't actually work, but still receives a paycheck.

size up - (id.) to make an estimation of or decision about the value or worth of something; (syn.) evaluate. e.g. - The town's people sized up the damage caused by the earthquake.

skirmish - (n.) a small fight in a war. e.g. - It was not a full-scale battle, but only a small skirmish.

skyrocket - (v.) to rapidly increase to an excessive amount. e.g. - The early frost in Florida has caused the price of oranges to skyrocket.

slander - (v.) to cause damage to an individual's reputation as a result of lying, rumors, or gossip. e.g. - You should not destroy his good name through such slander. Der. (n.) slander.

slash - (n.) a long, narrow cut; (syn.) slit. e.g. - She bled to death from the self-inflicted slashes on her wrists. Der. (v.) slash.

sleek - (adj.) having a smooth, bright surface. e.g. - The new motorcycle had a sleek surface as a result of the bright paint that had been applied to it. Der. (n.) sleekness; (v.) sleek; (adv.) sleekly.

slippery - (adj.) the quality of causing something to fall or change position as a result of being wet or moist. e.g. - Be careful when you walk on the floor. You might fall as I have just mopped it, and it might still be slippery. Der. (v.) slip.

slit - (n.) a long, narrow cut; (syn.) slash. e.g. - This envelope has been opened. It has a slit along the side. Der. (v.) slit.

slovenly - (adj.) unclean in behavior or appearance. e.g. - He looked slovenly in his dirty shoes and torn jeans.

sluggish - (adj.) slow in activity or movement. e.g. - The sluggish movement of the train caused its arrival to be delayed by one hour. Der. (adv.) sluggishly.

smear - (v.) to spread or rub out. e.g. - The glass was smeared with fingerprints and needed to be washed. Der. (n.) smear.

smother - (v.) to stop the breathing of another person by placing an object over the face, esp. a pillow. e.g. - The victim's breathing stopped when he was smothered with a pillow.

snag - (n.) problem or difficulty. e.g. - We experienced several snags on our vacation, including being robbed and losing our luggage. Der. (v.) snag.

sneaky - (adj.) relating to an individual who uses dishonesty or exploitation; sly; (syn.) cunning. e.g. - It was very sneaky of him to steal money from the people who had grown to trust him. Der. (n.) sneak; (v.) sneak.

snub - (v.) to shun or avoid socially. e.g. - She is a conceited woman and often snubs us in public when she is with her wealthy friends.

soak - (v.) to become full or covered with water or moisture; (syn.) drench. e.g. - The towel was soaked after we used it to wipe up the water.

sober - (adj.) being fully in control of one's faculties; not drunk. e.g. - Many accidents occur because some people are not sober when they drive.

solicit - (v.) to request; to attempt to acquire or obtain. e.g. - After being charged with murder, he solicited the advice of a lawyer. Der. (n.) solicitation.

spacious - (adj.) having enough room or space; (syn.) roomy. e.g. - Our house is quite spacious. It has seventeen rooms. Der. (n.) spaciousness; (adv.) spaciously.

spawn - (v.) to produce or cause to develop; to create. e.g. - His argumentative attitude often spawns many disagreements. Der. (n.) spawn.

specimen - (n.) a sample, esp. one used for purposes of examination. e.g. - The doctor took a blood specimen from my arm in order to determine the cause of my illness.

spill the beans - (id.) to divulge secret information. e.g. - She spilled the beans about all the confidential information that I had told her.

spine - (n.) the backbone. e.g. - He is paralyzed from the chest down as a result of an injury to the top part of his spine. Der. (adj.) spinal.

splinter - (n.) a small fragment of wood. e.g. - A piece of wood broke off of the table and left a splinter in my finger. Der. (adj.) splintered.

sponsor - (v.) to provide support or financing for a specific activity, esp. by an institution or organization. e.g. - Coca-Cola sponsored the Olympic Games by providing substantial financial support. Der. (n.) sponsor, sponsorship; (adj.) sponsored.

spring up - (id.) to appear quickly or unexpectedly from a specific source. e.g. - A leak suddenly sprang up from the water pipe.

sprout - (v.) to grow from a planted seed. e.g. - The first traces of greenery appeared through the soil as the seeds began to sprout. Der. (n.) sprout.

squalor - (n.) Many houses in the poor, run-down neighborhood exist in a state of squalor. Der. (adj.) squalid.

squat - (v.) to stand on one's feet, low to the ground, with the knees bent; (syn.) crouch. e.g. - He was squatting by the fireplace, trying to start the fire.

stack - (n.) a pile of items placed in a vertical position, one on the top of the other. e.g. - Huan had a stack of books on his desk that was two feet high. Der. (v.) stack; (adj.) stacked.

stagnant - (adj.) not moving; standing still. e.g. - The water in this lake is stagnant since it doesn't flow to another waterway. Der. (n.) stagnation; (v.) stagnate; (adv.) stagnantly.

stained - (adj.) to discolor cloth materials with dirt, food, or drink. e.g. - His jeans became grass-stained while playing baseball. Der. (n.) stain; (v.) stain.

stale - (adj.) lacking in freshness or flavor. e.g. - This bread is stale and is too hard to eat.

staunch - (adj.) relating to strength in one's beliefs or opinions. e.g. - He is a staunch supporter of the Republican Party and often donates money to their campaigns. Der. (adv.) staunchly.

steer clear of - (id.) to avoid. e.g. - If you steer clear of the dangerous areas when you are in New York City, you shouldn't have any problem.

stench - (n.) an offensive smell or odor. e.g. - Your dirty socks are giving off a stench. Why don't you wash them?

sthg under your hat - (id.) to hide a secret. e.g. - I don't trust him. He has something under his hat.

sthg up your sleeve - (id.) to hide information about something. e.g. - Is that all you wanted to tell me or do you have something up your sleeve?

stick to your guns - (id.) not changing one's mind or opinion. e.g. - He won't change his mind because he always sticks to his guns.

stick-in-the-mud - (id.) a person who is slow or old-fashioned in thinking. e.g. - He's such a stick-in-the-mud. He always wants to go to bed by 10:00.

sticky - (adj.)(1) covered with glue; adhesive. (2)(met.) a difficult or problematic situation. e.g. - (1) The adhesive tape was sticky on both sides. (2) He found himself in a sticky situation when his wife discovered that he was having an affair. Der. (n.) sticker; (v.) stick.

stifle - (v.) to suppress, discourage, or hold back. e.g. - Why do you always stifle me when I want to speak? I have the right to express my opinions.

stingy - (adj.) not generous with money or in spending. e.g. - He is so stingy that he insists on her paying whenever they go out. Der. (n.) stinginess; (adv.) stingily

stocky - (adj.) relating to men who have a short, muscular build. e.g. - Aaron is stocky because weight-lifting is his hobby.

stood up - (id.) to have an appointment or a date broken by someone. e.g. - I was supposed to meet Isaac at 10:00, but he stood me up.

stoop - (v.) to bend forward from the waist or shoulders. e.g. - The hiker stooped forward from the weight of his backpack.

stout - (adj.) strong and healthy. e.g. - The army captain was a stout man who was six feet tall and weighed 210 pounds. Der. (adv.) stoutly.

strand - (v.) to cause to be left alone, esp. in a vulnerable or dangerous situation. e.g. – Robinson Crusoe was stranded on a desert island and waited to be rescued. Der. (adj.) stranded.

strangle - (v.) to stop the breathing of another person by placing a rope or the hands around the neck. e.g. - The police investigation determined that the victim was strangled since her neck was bruised. Der. (n.) strangulation.

strapping - (adj.) very strong and healthy; (syn.) hearty. e.g. - Kerry is a strapping young man. He eats nutritious food and exercises every day.

strenuous - (adj.) demanding great physical strength or endurance. e.g. - Lifting the heavy box was a very strenuous task. Der. (adv.) strenuously.

strewn - (p. part.) spread; scattered; thrown about. e.g. - His bedroom was a mess. Everything was strewn about. Der. (v.) strew.

strife - (n.) conflict; friction. e.g. - There is a good deal of strife in Congress. Politicians are always arguing about differing viewpoints.

stringent - (adj.) strict or rigid. e.g. - Bruce's father has many stringent rules and often punishes him. Der. (adv.) stringently.

strip - (n.) an individual, thin piece of sthg. e.g. - The beef strips were grilled on the barbecue.

strive (for/to) - (v.) to attempt sthg with serious energy and effort. He is an excellent student and strives for perfection in all his homework assignments.

structure - (n.) a building. e.g. - The city has various structures, including office buildings, apartment buildings, and single-family homes. Der. (v.) structure; (adj.) structural.

studious - (adj.) relating to individuals who read or study extensively. e.g. - Shanti is very studious. She spends five hours a day doing her homework.

stuffy - (adj.) inflexible in following tradition or custom. e.g. - He is so stuffy that most people think he is inflexible and boring. Der. (n.) stuffiness; (adv.) stuffily.

stumbling block - (id.) something that prevents or hinders progress. (syn.) hindrance, obstacle, barrier. e.g. - His poor health was a stumbling block towards his performance at work.

stupendous - (adj.) amazing or astounding in size. e.g. - The circus was stupendous. It included one hundred different kinds of animals. Der. (adv.) stupendously.

sturdy - (adj.) relating to objects that are strong and solid. e.g. - This table is sturdy and can hold quite heavy objects. Der. (adv.) sturdily.

sty - (n.) a small house for a pig. e.g. - The pig was sleeping in its sty in order to be protected from the sunlight.

subdued - (adj.) to control or reduce in degree of feeling. e.g. - Hana was quite angry earlier in the week, but she's feeling more subdued now.

subject (to) - (v.) to force to experience or endure something, esp. something unpleasant or unwanted. e.g. - He was subjected to punishment from his father for arriving home late.

subjugate - (v.) to suppress or take control of. e.g. - The police attempted to subjugate the rioters. Der. (n.) subjugation.

submerge - (v.) to place an object under the surface of the water. e.g. - Katie frightened us when she submerged herself in the lake for three minutes. We were worried that she might have drowned. Der. (n.) submergence.

subordinate - (adj.) being less in rank or authority. e.g. - He has a subordinate position in the company. There are ten managers in authority over him. Der. (n.) subordination, subordinate; (v.) subordinate.

subscribe - (v.) to receive publications or services at regular time intervals in exchange for a fee. e.g. - Adam subscribes to *The New Yorker* and receives a magazine every month. Der. (n.) subscription; (n.) subscriber.

subsequent - (adj.) following in sequence, order, or time. e.g. - Subsequent to high school, he attended college. Der. (adv.) subsequently.

subside - (v.) to settle downwards. e.g. - The ground subsided during the earthquake. Geologists now estimate that it is three inches lower than before. Der. (n.) subsidence.

subsistence - (n.) the minimum amount of food necessary for human existence. e.g. - Children in certain countries in Africa do not have enough food for normal subsistence. Some of them are starving. Der. (v.) subsist.

subterfuge - (n.) trickery used in order free oneself from blame or responsibility. e.g. - The suspect's subterfuge consisted of telling the police that his identical twin brother had committed the crime.

sumptuous - (adj.) extremely rich in texture or quality. e.g. - The queen's palace had sumptuous decorations. Der. (n.) sumptuousness; (adv.) sumptuously.

supercilious - (adj.) arrogant; conceited. e.g. - He is the most supercilious person I know. He thinks he knows everything about everything. Der. (n.) superciliousness; (adv.) superciliously.

superficial - (adj.) not deep or profound; surface. e.g. - Debra is a superficial woman. Her only interests are clothes and make-up. Der. (adv.) superficially.

superfluous - (adj.) beyond what is necessary. e.g. - The teacher asked for a 300 word composition. Writing 1,000 words was totally superfluous. Der. (n.) superfluity; (adv.) superfluously.

supersede - (v.) to cause to become outdated as a result of being replaced. e.g. - That law is no longer effective as it has been superseded by a new law. Der. (n.) supersession.

superstition - (n.) a belief in supernatural powers or occurrences. e.g. - She believed in the superstition that black cats cause bad luck. Der. (adj.) superstitious; (adv.) superstitiously.

suppress - (v.) to cause to stop or prevent for a period of time. e.g. - This syrup will suppress your cough for three hours. Der. (n.) suppression, suppressant; (adj.) suppressed.

surge - (v.) to rise or move forward suddenly. e.g. - The fans, who had been waiting for hours, surged into the stadium when the gates were finally opened. Der. (n.) surge.

surplus - (n.) an excessive quantity, beyond what is required or necessary. e.g. - The army had a surplus of boots, which were stored in a warehouse.

suspect - (n.) an individual who has committed a crime. e.g. - He is a suspect in the crime since his fingerprints were found at the crime scene. Der. (v.) suspect.

sustenance - (n.) food; nourishment. e.g. - Healthy food and clean water are necessary for human sustenance. Der. (v.) sustain.

sweet tooth - (id.) to enjoy eating sweets very much. e.g. - He has a sweet tooth and enjoys eating cake and candy.

swelling - (n.) the increase in size of a bodily part as if filled by water. e.g. - The doctor recommended that we put ice on Timothy's twisted ankle to prevent swelling. Der. (v.) swell; (adj.) swollen.

swindler - (n.) an individual who acquires money through fraud or dishonesty. e.g. - Emma lost her life savings to a swindler who promised to invest her money, but later left town with all of it. Der. (v.) swindle.

Exercises – S

Instructions: Complete the sentences below, using one of the words beginning with the letter "S" from the previous section. Note that some gaps require a single word, while others may need a phrasal verb or idiomatic expression. You may also need to change the form of the word. The answers are provided at the end of book.

1) This meal is _____. It is truly delicious.

2) Because of _____ funding, the volunteer center had to be closed.

3) That water is _____. It is not fit to drink and is beginning to smell bad.

4) My accident caused a _____ to my studies, and I graduated a semester later.

5) You will appear _____ if you never clean your shoes or comb your hair.

6) It is going to be impossible to change her point of view. She always _____.

7) The anti-gravity capsule attempts to _____ flight in outer space.

8) Carrying 120 pounds of luggage through three airports was certainly a _____ task.

9) The political party leader is so _____. He is really corrupt, but he always talks about the importance of being honest.

10) The sales person was actually a _____ who promised to deliver the merchandise, but just took all the money instead.

Words – T

Instructions: Study the words below, paying attention to their meanings as well as how they are used in the example sentences. Then complete the exercise that follows.

tackle - (v.) to attempt with difficulty. e.g. - She put off doing her homework all weekend and finally tackled it on Sunday evening.

take its/their toll - (id.) to begin to affect, esp. negatively. e.g. - Missing several nights of sleep finally took its toll on him.

tale - (n.) a story, esp. one that is not based on the truth. e.g. - He told a tall tale which no one believed.

talk a mile a minute - (id.) to talk very quickly. e.g. - It is so difficult to understand him. He talks a mile a minute.

tangible - (adj.) being perceived by the senses; real; material. e.g. - The insensitive man valued his tangible possessions more than love or friendship. Der. (n.) tangibility; (adv.) tangibly.

tankard - (n.) a large cup or mug. e.g. - She drank the coffee from a large tankard.

tantamount (to) - (adj.) equal to in terms of results or consequences. e.g. - Refusing to tell the entire truth is tantamount to lying.

tap - (v.) to place small listening devices secretly on telephone lines. e.g. - The drug dealer made arrangements with his supplier only over public telephones since he suspected that his private telephone line had been tapped. Der. (n.) tap.

tardiness - (n.) lateness for school or work. e.g. - Jeff's tardiness at work has become a serious problem. He was warned that he will be fired the next time he's late. Der. (adj.) tardy.

tee totaling - (adj.) totally refraining from the consumption of alcoholic drinks. e.g. - Todd used to be an alcoholic, but now he is tee totaling and never drinks. Der. (v.) teetotal.

tedious - (adj.) monotonous or tiring. e.g. - Working in a factory assembly line is tedious work. Most factory workers suffer from boredom. Der. (n.) tedium; (adv.) tediously.

temperamental - (adj.) excessively sensitive or unpredictable in mood or state of mind. e.g. - Nathan is so temperamental that you never know what kind of mood he will be in. Der. (n.) temperament; (adv.) temperamentally.

temporal - (adj.) relating to sensual or earthly desires. e.g. - Monks are required to place little importance on temporal needs, such as food and clothing, in order to concentrate on spiritual concerns. Der. (n.) temporality; (adv.) temporally.

tenet - (n.) belief; doctrine; dogma. e.g. - One of the basic tenets of mathematics is that any unknown quantity can be calculated by using the proper equation.

terse - (adj.) unnecessarily brief or abrupt in speech. e.g. - Mia was so terse this morning. When I asked her how she was, she told me that is was none of my business. Der. (n.) terseness; (adv.) tersely.

testament - (n.) written proof relating to the disposal of property after an individual's death. e.g. - An individual's last will and testament is often read after the funeral in order to determine how property should be distributed.

testify - (v.) to make a statement in court under oath. e.g. - Brittney witnessed the bank robbery and must testify in court about what she saw take place. Der. (n.) testimony; (n.) testimonial.

texture - (n.) the quality of the surface or structure of something. The texture of the blanket was soft and fuzzy. Der. (v.) texturize.

That takes the cake! - (id.) that is shocking or unbelievable. e.g. - He asked to borrow money from you again. That really takes the cake!

That's the way the cookie crumbles - (id.) That's life. e.g. - I just lost ten dollars. Oh well, that's the way the cookie crumbles.

thaw - (v.) to return a frozen object to its normal temperature. e.g. - The frozen meat needs to be removed from the freezer and thawed before it can be cooked. Der. (adj.) thawed.

throng - (n.) a crowd or large gathering of people. e.g. - A noisy throng of 100,000 spectators was present at the basketball championship. Der. (v.) throng.

thwart - (v.) to oppose, prevent, hinder, or frustrate. e.g. - His poor health thwarted his progress in school.

tilt - (v.) to move or lean towards one side. e.g. - The repairman tilted the machine to one side in order to fix it. Der. (n.) tilt; (adj.) tilted.

timid - (adj.) shy; easily embarrassed. e.g. - Parveen is so timid that she is afraid to speak. Der. (n.) timidity; (adv.) timidly.

tiny - (adj.) very small; (syn.) dinky, puny. e.g. - The bug was so tiny that it could hardly be seen.

tipsy - (adj.) dizzy or euphoric, esp. from drunkenness. She felt tipsy after having drunk the bottle of wine. Der. (n.) tipsiness; (adv.) tipsily.

toe the line - (id.) to conform to a rigid standard of behavior. e.g. - If you want to lose ten pounds in two weeks, you will have to toe the line.

token - (n.) an indication or display of appreciation. e.g. - Please accept this gift as a token of my appreciation for all the help you've given me.

tolerate - (v.) to possess the ability to accept or endure another person's behavior, esp. when it is offensive or undesirable. e.g. - I don't really enjoy his company, but I can tolerate him sometimes.

topple - (v.) to cause to fall down. e.g. - Many buildings toppled to the ground during the earthquake.

touch base - (id.) to come into contact or communicate with. e.g. - I will touch base with you next week concerning the status of the contract.

touchy - (id.) overly sensitive or moody. e.g. - She is touchy and hates being criticized.

trail - (n.) a small dirt road that is formed by the movement of traffic or people. e.g. - The hikers walked along the trail through the woods. Der. (v.) trail.

transplant - (n.) the replacement of a bodily organ with another organ from a deceased person. e.g. - The patient's diseased liver was replaced during the transplant operation. Der. (v.) transplant.

treacherous - (adj.) dangerous; (syn.) precarious. e.g. - The weather is treacherous today. Travel is not advised. Der. (n.) treacherousness, treachery; (adv.) treacherously.

treason - (n.) the action of disloyalty or betrayal towards an individual's government of nationality or citizenship. e.g. - The American politician was accused of treason for revealing military secrets.

treaty - (n.) an agreement made between or among two or more nations. e.g. - An import/export treaty exists between the U.S. and Japan.

trench - (n.) a long, narrow area that has been dug in the ground; ditch. e.g. - During World War I, soldiers often fought while standing in trenches for protection. Der. (v.) entrench.

trend - (n.) the current preference displayed by the public; tendency. e.g. - Current economic trends show increased activity in the marketplace. Der. (adj.) trendy.

tributary - (n.) a river which enters a larger river or lake. e.g. - The Missouri River is a tributary of the Mississippi River as it flows into the Mississippi at St. Louis.

trim - (v.) to cut at the edges. e.g. - Hong had her hair trimmed by the hairdresser. She had only an inch cut off. Der. (n.) trim.

troop - (n.) a unit of soldiers in the armed services. e.g. - The troop of soldiers set up camp for the evening.

trunk - (n.) the central wooden part of a tree from which branches grow. e.g. - A tree will fall down if it is cut through the trunk.

trying - (adj.) physically, mentally, or psychologically demanding; (syn.) arduous; enervating. e.g. - Aiko finds her boss's complaints and demands very trying.

turbulent - (adj.) causing the development of violence or disturbance. e.g. - The turbulent atmosphere in the city is a result of disharmony among various races. Der. (n.) turbulence.

turn on a dime - (id.) to have great flexibility in motion. e.g. - This car is one of the finest machines I have ever driven. It can turn on a dime.

turn over a new leaf - (id.) to improve one's behavior; to change for the better. e.g. - The student promised to turn over a new leaf and start handing in his homework on time.

twig - (n.) a small piece on the branch of a tree. e.g. - Several small twigs were gathered from the forest to start the campfire.

Exercises – T

Instructions: Complete the sentences below, using one of the words beginning with the letter "T" from the previous section. Note that some gaps require a single word, while others may need a phrasal verb or idiomatic expression. You may also need to change the form of the word. The answers are provided at the end of book.

1) You have to _____ in court if you see a crime take place.

2) Her job is difficult and _____. She has thought about quitting many times.

3) We finally _____ the unpleasant task last weekend.

4) The child promised _____ and start behaving better.

5) Saying that you aren't that fond of her is _____ to saying that you really don't like her.

6) His house and car were the _____ indications of his success in life.

7) _____ for class will not be tolerated. Students will have to report to the principal if they are late to class.

8) Artists can be _____ and sensitive to criticism about their work.

9) The _____ of her skin was smooth and silky.

10) A loud _____ of one thousand people started the protest.

Words – U to V

Instructions: Study the words below, paying attention to their meanings as well as how they are used in the example sentences. Then complete the exercise that follows.

ultimatum - (n.) the action of being presented with two difficult or undesirable choices. e.g. - The student received the ultimatum that he would be expelled if his grades did not improve.

unanimous - (adj.) relating to full and total agreement by all members of a group. e.g. - The new law received the unanimous support of all members of Congress. Der. (n.) unanimity; (adv.) unanimously.

unconventional - (adj.) non-traditional; very unusual or eccentric. e.g. - Monica is a very unconventional woman. She has many unusual habits. Der. (adv.) unconventionally.

undaunted - (adj.) courageous; not afraid or discouraged by opposition or adversity. e.g. - The soldier was undaunted in spite of the danger he faced in battle. Der. (v.) daunt.

undemonstrative - (adj.) not displaying feeling or emotion. e.g. - Mark is so undemonstrative that we couldn't tell whether he was happy or not. Der. (adv.) undemonstratively.

under the weather - (id.) to feel sick or generally unwell. e.g. - He feels under the weather and has been in bed for four days.

underdeveloped - (adj.) inadequate in terms of preparation, growth, or strength. e.g. My brother is so underdeveloped for his age that he is almost a foot shorter than the other boys in his class. Der. (n.) underdevelopment; (ant.) developed.

undermine - (v.) to weaken gradually. e.g. - His health was undermined by the progression of the disease. Der. (adj.) undermined.

undertaking - (n.) a project, enterprise, or job, especially one of significant size or effort. e.g. - Painting a fifteen-room house in a day was a huge undertaking. Der. (n.) undertake.

undoing - (n.) ruin; destruction; demise. e.g. - Drug abuse was his undoing. He lost his family, his job, and his home.

uniformity - (n.) similarity in size, shape, weight, or quality. e.g. - The factory strives for uniformity in quality of all the goods it manufactures. Der. (adv.) uniform. Der. (adv.) uniformly.

unsavory - (adj.) distasteful; (syn.) insipid. e.g. - This soup is unsavory and isn't fit to eat. Der. (ant.) savory.

unscrupulous - (adj.) without honest or integrity. e.g. - She lost all her money in an unscrupulous business arrangement. Der. (n.) unscrupulousness; (adv.) unscrupulously.

unwavering - (adj.) constant; unchanging. e.g. - He had always been a football fanatic. His enthusiasm for the sport is unwavering.

up to doing sthg - (id.) to be in the mood to do something. e.g. - I'm not up to going out tonight. Let's stay home.

upheaval - (n.) the action of causing disturbance or disorder. e.g. - He always causes upheaval in the class with his constant interruptions. Der. (v.) upheave.

utmost - (adj.) the highest or greatest aspect of something. e.g. - Brushing your teeth daily is of the utmost importance for good dental hygiene.

vacillate - (v.) to waver back and forth between alternative choices. e.g. - She continued to vacillate between the two choices and was unable to make a decision. Der. (n.) vacillation; (adj.) vacillated, vacillating; (adv.) vacillatingly.

valiantly - (adv.) being done with strength, bravery, and determination; heroically. e.g. - The fireman died valiantly in the blaze, saving the life of a small child. Der. (adj.) valiant.

variation - (n.) change or alteration. e.g. – My father does not like change. He gets upset if there is any variation in his normal daily routine. Der. (n.) variance; (v.) vary; (adj.) varied.

vault - (1)(n.) a burial chamber; (2)(n.) a place used for storing valuables. e.g. - (1) The bodies of murder victims are often stored in vaults which may be re-opened in the event that further examinations are necessary. (2) The millionaire stored his money and other valuables in a vault.

ventilation - (n.) the action of receiving sufficient air or oxygen. e.g.- The window was opened so that the room could receive some ventilation. Der. (v.) ventilate; (adj.) ventilated.

venture - (n.) a business arrangement involving risk or speculation. e.g. - Gambling at Las Vegas can be a dangerous venture.

venue - (n.) the place or location at which an event takes place. e.g. - The stadium is the venue for the concert.

verdict - (n.) decision by a jury in court. e.g. - If the jury returns a verdict of guilty at the end of a trial, the suspect will be sent to prison.

verify - (v.) to determine the truth of. e.g. - A lie detector test is often used to verify the details of statements given by suspects. Der. (n.) verification, verity; veracity (adj.) verified.

versatile - (adj.) possessing many skills, talents, or uses. e.g. - My niece is a very versatile musician. She knows how to play the piano and guitar and can also sing beautifully. Der. (n.) versatility.

vessel - (n.) a ship or boat. e.g. - He owns an expensive yacht. It is really an amazing vessel and has the most modern equipment.

vicious - (adj.) relating to the desire to cause harm or injury; cruel. e.g. - The lies you said about my mother were vicious. You only wanted to hurt me. Der. (n.) viciousness; (adv.) viciously.

vicissitude - (n.) a change in a situation or circumstance, generally for the worse. e.g. - There have been many vicissitudes in the economy this year, including a rise in unemployment and an increase in the rate of inflation. Der. (n.) vicissitudinous.

victuals - (n.)(also vittles) food. e.g. - Our victuals are stored in the refrigerator and kitchen cupboards.

vie - (v.) to engage in competition or rivalry. e.g. - The two teams will vie for the championship on Sunday.

vigilant - exercising extreme care or caution in outlook. e.g. - The doctors were vigilant in watching the president after his heart attack. Der. (n.) vigilance; (adv.) vigilantly.

villain - (n.) dishonest person; criminal; crook. e.g. - The villain cheated the elderly couple out of their life savings. Der. (v.) vilify.

vindication - (n.) the action of seeking revenge or setting free from blame. e.g. - His vindication from the charge of murder came when the judge announced that he was not guilty. Der. (v.) vindicate.

violation - (n.) offense; crime. e.g. - It is a violation of traffic laws to drive a car after dark without turning its lights on. Der. (v.) violate.

virile - (adj.) the quality of being full of strength and energy. e.g. - The virile weight-lifter managed to lift seven hundred pounds.

vital - (adj.) very important or necessary. e.g. - Studying is vital if you want to do well on your final examinations. Der. (adv.) vitally.

vocational - (adj.) relating to training or education in a particular skill or craft. e.g. - The college offers many vocational courses, including woodworking and automotive repair. Der. (n.) vocation.

voluble - (adj.) very talkative. e.g. - My best friend is so voluble that she is almost always talking.

voluntarily - (adv.) being done by free choice, without external pressure or influence. e.g. - My neighbor works at the local hospital voluntarily three times a week, even though he receives no payment for his services. Der. (n.) volunteer; (v.) volunteer; (adj.) voluntary.

vow - (n.) promise. e.g. - During the marriage ceremony, the groom made a vow to be faithful to his wife until death. Der. (v.) vow.

vulgar - (adj.) offensive in content or expression; lewd; in bad taste. e.g. - Many CDs have warnings because their songs contain vulgar lyrics. Der. (n.) vulgarity.

Exercises – U to V

Instructions: Complete the sentences below, using one of the words beginning with the letters "U" to "V" from the previous section. Note that some gaps require a single word, while others may need a phrasal verb or idiomatic expression. You may also need to change the form of the word. The answers are provided at the end of book.

1) He _____ between two versions of the story, so it was impossible to tell which one was true.

2) The progress of the construction of the building was _____ by the poor weather.

3) If the jury returns a _____ of innocent, the suspect will be released.

4) Adopting a child is an incredible _____. So much responsibility is involved in raising a child.

5) The management of that company is very _____. I have never heard of any other company that permits employees to sleep on the job.

6) The auditorium is the _____ for the graduation ceremony.

7) _____ in the economy have caused many companies to go out of business in recent years.

8) I gave my boyfriend the _____ that I would leave him if he continued to flirt with other women.

9) Her love for her children is _____. Nothing could change her feelings.

10) Using profanity, swearing, and spitting are _____ habits.

Words W to Z

Instructions: Study the words below, paying attention to their meanings as well as how they are used in the example sentences. Then complete the exercise that follows.

wag - (v.) the side-to-side motion made by a dog's tail. e.g. - The happy dog stood by the road wagging its tail. Der. (n.) wag.

ward - (n.) an individual under custody or guardianship. e.g. - The orphaned child had no living relatives and became a ward of the state, which provided food and shelter.

warp - (v.) to cause wood to become disfigured as a result of exposure to water or moisture. e.g. - The surface of the table top is not level. The water leaking from the ceiling has warped it. Der. (adj.) warped. Der. (n.) warp.

wary - (adj.) cautious because of concerns or worries about something, especially about safety. e.g. - He was very wary of traveling through such a bad neighborhood. Der. (n.) wariness; (adv.) warily.

wayward - (adj.) being done contrary to the expectations of society or others. e.g. - Maria was a wayward adolescent. She helped rob a bank when she was just thirteen.

weary - (adj.) very tired. e.g. - The trip lasted thirty-two hours and the travelers were quite weary from the journey. Der. (adv.) wearily.

whim - (n.) a sudden or eccentric idea or impulse. e.g. - She dyed her hair bright purple on a whim. Der. (adj.) whimsical.

whip - (n.) a device consisting of a handle and a long leather strap, used for the purpose of torturing or beating. e.g. - The farmer used the whip to strike the horse in order to move it forward. Der. (v.) whip.

wholesome - (adj.) acceptable in terms of health, character, or morals. e.g. - Milk is a wholesome drink because it is full of vitamins and minerals. Der. (n.) wholesomeness.

widespread - (adj.) existing or extending over a wide area or region; extensive. e.g. - Drug addiction is so widespread that it is now a very serious problem in every American city.

winsome - (adj.) charming; pleasant; cheerful; (syn.) affable, amiable, cordial. e.g. - Jane is a very winsome girl. She is rarely unhappy.

wistful - (adj.) causing sadness or depression. e.g. - Alison felt wistful when her marriage ended, and she went into a deep depression. Der. (adv.) wistfully.

wither - (v.) to lack freshness as a result of becoming dried out. e.g. - If you don't put those flowers in some water, they will wither. Der. (adj.) withered.

witness - (n.) an individual who saw a crime being committed. e.g. - Yuki was a witness to the car accident. She saw it happen when she was standing across the street. Der. (v.) witness.

witty - (adj.) amusing and intelligent. e.g. - Mohammed told a witty joke which made us all laugh. Der. (n.) wit; (adv.) wittily.

wrath - (n.) anger. e.g. - You will suffer the wrath of your parents if you disobey them.

wretched - (adj.) being particularly bad in quality; (syn.) dismal. e.g. - The team's performance was wretched and, of course, they lost the game. Der. (n.) wretchedness; (adv.) wretchedly.

yank - (v.) to pull suddenly and forcefully. e.g. - The door was stuck and we had to yank it in order to open it.

yearn - (v.) to crave or desire. e.g. - Having grown tired of city life, William yearned for a life in the country. Der. (n.) yearning.

you can count on it - (id.) you can depend on it; it is certain to happen. e.g. - You can count on her coming to the party. She promised to be there.

zealot - (n.) an individual displaying unreasonable enthusiasm; fanatic. e.g. - Susan is an absolute zealot about her exercise routine. She goes to the gym twice a day. Der. (adj.) zealous; (adv.) zealously.

Exercises – W to Z

Instructions: Complete the sentences below, using one of the words beginning with the letters "W" to "Z" from the previous section. Note that some gaps require a single word, while others may need a phrasal verb or idiomatic expression. You may also need to change the form of the word. The answers are provided at the end of book.

1) He was _____ of beginning the journey when it was raining so heavily.

2) She is a _____ about keeping the house clean. She cleans it every day.

3) These fresh herbs will _____ if it is too hot in the kitchen.

4) I felt absolutely _____ yesterday. I couldn't even get out of bed

5) He couldn't take care of himself because of his health and financial problems, and he finally had to become a _____ of the state

6) She _____ the accident and had to tell the police officer what she had seen.

7) She is such a _____ person. She tells such funny jokes.

8) Having been away from home for a year, Yoko _____ to see her family.

9) She was so _____ when she moved and had to say goodbye to all her good friends.

10) Those who fail to follow social norms will suffer the _____ of society.

Answers – A:

1) affiliation
2) accompany
3) animosity
4) arduous
5) accessible
6) adhesive
7) adversaries
8) alibi
9) alluded
10) ambiance

Answers – B:

1) beating around the bush
2) bills
3) breach
4) buoys
5) broke down
6) bland
7) belittles
8) baffled
9) blandishment
10) bored to tears

Answers – D:

1) chortled
2) capsized
3) cavity
4) clutter
5) clandestine
6) collaboration
7) classifies
8) capitulated
9) charming
10) cogent

Answers – D:

1) dense
2) despicable
3) diligent
4) dismantled
5) diversified
6) downfall
7) dysfunction
8) dingy
9) desperation
10) defect

Answers – E:

1) elusive
2) enervating
3) enterprises
4) exacerbate
5) extenuating
6) entails
7) effigy
8) eerie
9) embezzling
10) endeavor

Answers – F:

1) facetious
2) flanked
3) fortuitous
4) frivolous
5) fundamental
6) fulsome
7) flourish
8) foiled
9) frolicking
10) fizzle out

Answers – G to H:

1) get in touch

2) garnishes

3) handy

4) grumbles

5) grasping at straws

6) hoarse

7) hit the spot

8) hunch

9) garbled

10) hushed

Answers – I:

1) immaculate

2) implicated or incriminated

3) in the red

4) inhabitant

5) impeccable

6) instigated

7) idle

8) implored

9) indefatigable

10) impact

Answers – J to L:

1) jotted down

2) latent

3) loquacious

4) knack

5) jumble

6) label

7) luxurious

8) liabilities

9) licentious

10) jurisdiction

Answers – M to O:

1) obliterated

2) nominated

3) obstinate

4) overabundance

5) nit-picks

6) magnanimity

7) noxious

8) mandatory

9) ostentatious

10) mitigated

Answers – P:

1) phlegmatic

2) pillaged

3) peak

4) pioneer

5) precarious or prostrate

6) putrid

7) playing with fire

8) protracted

9) perceptible

10) pull through

Answers – Q to R:

1) rehabilitation

2) render

3) quaint

4) recuperate

5) quest

6) relinquish

7) recruitment

8) quirk

9) retrospect

10) reluctant

Answers – S:

1) scrumptious

2) scant

3) stagnant

4) setback

5) slovenly

6) sticks to her guns

7) simulate

8) strenuous

9) sanctimonious

10) swindler

Answers – T:

1) testify

2) trying or tedious

3) tackled

4) to turn over a new leaf

5) tantamount

6) tangible

7) tardiness

8) touchy

9) texture

10) throng

Answers – U to V:

1) vacillated

2) undermined

3) verdict

4) undertaking

5) unconventional

6) venue

7) vicissitudes

8) ultimatum

9) unwavering

10) vulgar

Answers – W to Z:

1) wary

2) zealot

3) wither

4) wretched

5) ward

6) witnessed

7) witty

8) yearned

9) wistful

10) wrath

VOCABULARY PRACTICE TEST 1

1. Farming and raising animals are important for the domestic economy.
   A. state
   B. national
   C. county
   D. annual

2. The child was gnawing his candy.
   A. sucking
   B. eating
   C. chewing
   D. swallowing

3. There have been some pervasive changes to the school's curriculum.
   A. extensive
   B. admirable
   C. difficult
   D. approved

4. It is often said that a person can be conspicuous by his or her absence.
   A. unaware
   B. acknowledged
   C. concealed
   D. noticeable

5. She said she didn't have the inclination to go out tonight.
   A. money
   B. desire
   C. time
   D. availability

6. No matter what we said, he was impervious to our suggestions.
   A. humiliated by
   B. critical of
   C. incapable of
   D. unaffected by

7. Traveling on that winding road into town is treacherous.
   A. dangerous
   B. ill-advised
   C. exciting
   D. tiring

8. The court case is surrounded by a(n) labyrinth of counterclaims.
   A. excess
   B. abundance
   C. maze
   D. puzzle

9. Elderly people are often prone to broken bones.
   A. troubled by
   B. vulnerable to
   C. afraid of
   D. overwhelmed by

10. The criminal had no contrition for his crimes.
    A. verdict
    B. punishment
    C. confession
    D. remorse

11. She had superficial injuries from the accident.
    A. ugly
    B. unexpected
    C. bloody
    D. slight

12. He will spend twenty years in prison for his involvement in illicit activities.
    A. unlawful
    B. imprudent
    C. shameful
    D. harmful

13. He has had a(n) illustrious career in the military.
    A. respectful
    B. outstanding
    C. elusive
    D. earnest

14. She needs to surmount her problems in order to get ahead in life.
    A. learn from
    B. endure
    C. overcome
    D. forget

15. Our lack of money is no obstacle towards finishing the project.
    A. facilitation
    B. assistance
    C. significance
    D. hindrance

16. He is a(n) layperson on that subject.
    A. amateur
    B. expert
    C. disinterested party
    D. academic

17. In order to be a good parent, one must foster a caring attitude.
    A. display
    B. adopt
    C. demonstrate
    D. present

18. Consensus most nearly means:
    A. discussion
    B. unanimity
    C. agreement
    D. harmony

19. Jeopardy most nearly means:
    A. chance
    B. danger
    C. insecurity
    D. unprotected

20. Elaborate most nearly means:
    A. unusual
    B. artificial
    C. invented
    D. extensive

21. Abate most nearly means:
    A. lessen
    B. lighten
    C. relinquish
    D. subdue

22. Sublime most nearly means:
    A. sensitive
    B. unforgettable
    C. excessive
    D. wonderful

23. Pithy most nearly means:
    A. absurd
    B. bitter
    C. brief
    D. weak

24. Livid most nearly means:
    A. upset
    B. furious
    C. annoyed
    D. emotional

25. Ruthless most nearly means:
    A. terrible
    B. obnoxious
    C. unkind
    D. cruel

26. Supplicate most nearly means:
    A. beg
    B. complain
    C. ask
    D. communicate

27. Abscond most nearly means:
    A. rob
    B. blackmail
    C. avoid capture
    D. dissipate

28. Paradox most nearly means:
    A. ambiguity
    B. enigma
    C. riddle
    D. contradiction

29. Subordinate most nearly means:
    A. unequal
    B. junior
    C. minor
    D. unnecessary

30. Fathom most nearly means:
    A. comprehend
    B. complicate
    C. recognize
    D. assess

31. Burnished most nearly means:
    A. waxed
    B. on fire
    C. polished
    D. engraved

32. Contaminate most nearly means:
    A. dump
    B. pollute
    C. harm
    D. filthy

33. <u>Intrepid</u> most nearly means:
    A. steadfast
    B. ambulatory
    C. adventurous
    D. fearless

34. <u>Predilection</u> most nearly means:
    A. preference
    B. perversion
    C. benediction
    D. antipathy

35. <u>Semblance</u> most nearly means:
    A. approximation
    B. attitude
    C. appearance
    D. awareness

VOCABULARY PRACTICE TEST 2

1. I wouldn't keep company with a(n) unsavory character like him.
   A. domineering
   B. awkward
   C. distasteful
   D. overbearing

2. The situation was fraught with stress and tension.
   A. full
   B. obvious
   C. plain
   D. clandestine

3. His day was filled with mundane tasks.
   A. frivolous
   B. obsequious
   C. interesting
   D. ordinary

4. Pandemic most nearly means:
   A. illness
   B. infection
   C. incidence
   D. outbreak

5. The two counties are contiguous.
   A. catching
   B. adjoining
   C. infectious
   D. cordial

6. The newspaper article reviled the new law.
   A. renewed
   B. reappraised
   C. evaluated
   D. criticized

7. Supercilious most nearly means:
   A. conceited
   B. ridiculous
   C. impervious
   D. ridiculed

8. We need to keep the rope taut.
   A. coiled
   B. tense
   C. submerged
   D. level

9. He went to Hollywood on a(n) whim.
   A. trip
   B. desire
   C. impulse
   D. jaunt

10. He has several lucrative businesses.
    A. consolidated
    B. financial
    C. time-consuming
    D. profitable

11. Opulent most nearly means:
    A. luxurious
    B. palatial
    C. expensive
    D. decadent

12. Inamorata most nearly means:
    A. boyfriend
    B. girlfriend
    C. spouse
    D. husband

13. A(n) treaty exists between the United States and the United Kingdom.
    A. boycott
    B. contract
    C. treatise
    D. agreement

14. This suitcase is very sturdy and should last a long time.
    A. heavy
    B. useful
    C. strong
    D. inimical

15. Rancid most nearly means:
    A. putrid
    B. unpleasant
    C. impure
    D. rampant

16. Maria was caught in a sudden deluge.
    A. downpour
    B. ambush
    C. storm
    D. crevice

17. This is a portrait of an eminent politician.
    A. disreputable
    B. distinguished
    C. impending
    D. forthcoming

18. He gave us a(n) eloquent speech at the ceremony.
    A. grandiose
    B. wordy
    C. staunch
    D. articulate

19. Fallible most nearly means:
    A. foolproof
    B. unacceptable
    C. errant
    D. diminished

20. There is rapport between the two countries.
    A. treaty
    B. harmony
    C. embargo
    D. communication

21. Embonpoint most nearly means:
    A. plumpness
    B. revealed
    C. attacked
    D. elegant

22. All of the passengers perished.
    A. waited
    B. disappeared
    C. boarded
    D. died

23. Impartial most nearly means:
    A. equanimity
    B. magnanimity
    C. fair
    D. biased

24. We have been asked to peruse the statue.
    A. interpret
    B. read
    C. assess
    D. file

25. Vital most nearly means the opposite of:
    A. unnecessary
    B. sentient
    C. lively
    D. essential

26. Conducive most nearly means:
    A. beneficial
    B. electrical
    C. circuitous
    D. regulated

27. Elite most nearly means:
    A. ludicrous
    B. exclusive
    C. enlightened
    D. costly

28. Barrier most nearly means:
    A. gateway
    B. crossroads
    C. impediment
    D. enforcement

29. Overtone most nearly means:
    A. proposition
    B. invitation
    C. advancement
    D. suggestion

30. Sumptuous most nearly means:
    A. audacious
    B. pretentious
    C. substantial
    D. luxurious

31. Indelible most nearly means the opposite of:
    A. unforgettable
    B. spoiled
    C. tasteless
    D. impermanent

32. Aghast most nearly means:
    A. undaunted
    B. appalled
    C. apprehensive
    D. unsurprised

33. Conflagration most nearly means:
    A. beating
    B. flailing
    C. inferno
    D. mishap

34. Barrage most nearly means:
    A. vessel
    B. initiative
    C. bombardment
    D. artillery

35. Fecund most nearly means:
    A. luscious
    B. favorable
    C. infertile
    D. productive

VOCABULARY PRACTICE TEST 3

1. Their company fabricates wooden sheds.
   A. designs
   B. assembles
   C. dismantles
   D. exports

2. Please put it in the receptacle when you are finished.
   A. appliance
   B. display
   C. wastebasket
   D. mailbox

3. Students should learn the rudimentary aspects of English grammar.
   A. fundamental
   B. advanced
   C. important
   D. problematic

4. He was a scrappy youngster.
   A. orphaned
   B. small
   C. poorly-dressed
   D. aggressive

5. He was told that the message was imperative.
   A. calamitous
   B. verbose
   C. indecipherable
   D. urgent

6. The specific details of the plan remained covert to the group.
   A. undisclosed
   B. loquacious
   C. terse
   D. private

7. Tony was a precocious child.
   A. unruly
   B. talented
   C. outspoken
   D. magnanimous

8. Her problems were insurmountable.
   A. pervasive
   B. troublesome
   C. insuperable
   D. exaggerated

9. The building was razed in three days.
   A. occupied
   B. finished
   C. constructed
   D. demolished

10. His countenance seemed to indicate that he was depressed.
    A. expression
    B. mood
    C. posture
    D. temperament

11. He has such a strange appellation.
    A. habit
    B. name
    C. quirk
    D. appearance

12. She was convicted of perjury.
    A. lying
    B. stealing
    C. perfidy
    D. contempt

13. Inventing the new machine involved a(n) immense amount of research and development.
    A. assiduous
    B. duplicitous
    C. indigent
    D. enormous

14. The hospital has recently received a(n) endowment.
    A. faculty
    B. gift
    C. resource
    D. loan

15. Darren is quite deft at using the computer.
    A. unskilled
    B. adept
    C. educated
    D. cogent

16. He is facing a predicament right now.
    A. dilemma
    B. obstacle
    C. inquiry
    D. decision

17. He has contended with many problems in his life.
    A. ignored
    B. procured
    C. managed
    D. brought on

18. The store was inundated with customers.
    A. overwhelmed by
    B. occupied by
    C. lacking in
    D. dealing with

19. Maladroit most nearly means:
    A. evil
    B. villainous
    C. difficult
    D. clumsy

20. Immerse most nearly means:
    A. dampen
    B. plunge
    C. extensive
    D. colossal

21. Sanction most nearly means:
    A. purge
    B. punish
    C. approve
    D. endorse

22. Feasible most nearly means:
    A. inappropriate
    B. impractical
    C. achievable
    D. trustworthy

23. Vanquish most nearly means:
    A. cleanse
    B. remove
    C. defeat
    D. demolish

24. Complacent most nearly means:
    A. self-satisfied
    B. forgetful
    C. exhausted
    D. lazy

25. Detrimental most nearly means:
    A. pointless
    B. unhealthy
    C. heedless
    D. harmful

26. Compendious most nearly means:
    A. capable
    B. comprehensive
    C. pendent
    D. published

27. Dwindle most nearly means:
    A. arise
    B. descend
    C. enhance
    D. diminish

28. Florescent most nearly means:
    A. alight
    B. glowing
    C. flowering
    D. growing

29. Canny most nearly means:
    A. shrewd
    B. alike
    C. frightening
    D. surprising

30. Accost most nearly means:
    A. detain
    B. attack
    C. imprison
    D. torture

31. Savory most nearly means:
    A. edible
    B. warm
    C. heated
    D. tasty

32. Larceny most nearly means:
    A. theft
    B. deception
    C. shoplifting
    D. criminal

33. Illusion most nearly means:
    A. implication
    B. viewpoint
    C. misapprehension
    D. day dream

34. Lethargic most nearly means:
    A. inattentive
    B. sluggish
    C. laid-back
    D. introverted

35. Novice most nearly means:
    A. non-expert
    B. trainee
    C. cadet
    D. beginner

VOCABULARY PRACTICE TEST 4

1. What you said really <u>intrigues</u> me.
   A. fulfils
   B. appalls
   C. fascinates
   D. subjugates

2. <u>Fatality</u> most nearly means:
   A. death
   B. disinclination
   C. accident
   D. injury

3. Paula has a(n) <u>penchant</u> for collecting antiques.
   A. insinuation
   B. preference
   C. indifference
   D. dissension

4. <u>Implicit</u> most nearly means:
   A. understood
   B. accurate
   C. hidden
   D. unstated

5. His response was <u>incoherent</u>.
   A. unenthusiastic
   B. muffled
   C. incomprehensible
   D. breathless

6. <u>Facilitate</u> most nearly means:
   A. teach
   B. assist
   C. construct
   D. rectify

7. He arrived at the airport <u>incognito</u>.
   A. late
   B. as expected
   C. in disguise
   D. punctually

8. <u>Encompass</u> most nearly means:
   A. involve
   B. anticipate
   C. measure
   D. navigate

9. She has such a <u>strident</u> voice.
   A. kind
   B. loud
   C. sweet
   D. hoarse

10. <u>Verify</u> most nearly means:
    A. conceal
    B. testify
    C. authenticate
    D. demonstrate

11. Knitting and other crafts have experienced a(n) revival recently.
    A. decline
    B. resurgence
    C. awakening
    D. setback

12. Haughty most nearly means:
    A. conceited
    B. breathless
    C. poorly-behaved
    D. ill-mannered

13. The marine displayed great mettle.
    A. skill
    B. courage
    C. adroitness
    D. obedience

14. Jovial most nearly means:
    A. supportive
    B. caring
    C. sincere
    D. cheerful

15. Everyone thought that the accident was ghastly.
    A. unforeseen
    B. serious
    C. hideous
    D. fatal

16. Flounder most nearly means:
    A. go swimming
    B. go fishing
    C. struggle
    D. disbelieve

17. The economy has recently been bolstered by an increase in interest rates.
    A. incited
    B. strengthened
    C. let down
    D. weakened

18. Acuity most nearly means:
    A. precision
    B. illness
    C. ignorance
    D. sensitivity

19. With hindsight, I can see things more clearly now.
    A. with experience
    B. with regret
    C. in remembrance
    D. in retrospect

20. Rigid most nearly means:
    A. stressed
    B. enclosed
    C. unbending
    D. unnerving

21. His father's death precipitated his decision.
    A. hastened
    B. prevented
    C. changed
    D. overcame

22. Lustrous most nearly means:
    A. expensive
    B. shiny
    C. cleansed
    D. shampooed

23. Furor most nearly means:
    A. leader
    B. commander
    C. sorrow
    D. outcry

24. Earnest most nearly means the opposite of:
    A. masculine
    B. athletic
    C. insincere
    D. capable

25. Arcanum most nearly means:
    A. ancient
    B. discrete
    C. dome
    D. mystery

26. Slander most nearly means:
    A. gossip
    B. defame
    C. refute
    D. lie

27. Unblemished most nearly means:
    A. faultless
    B. hygienic
    C. sparking
    D. indefinite

28. Wholesome most nearly means the opposite of:
    A. unhealthful
    B. disingenuous
    C. salutary
    D. salubrious

29. Adept most nearly means:
    A. efficient
    B. awkward
    C. skilled
    D. inept

30. Prosperous most nearly means:
    A. advanced
    B. prolific
    C. unfavorable
    D. successful

31. Salvage most nearly means:
    A. deliver
    B. save
    C. barbaric
    D. uncivilized

32. Valiant most nearly means:
    A. upper-class
    B. extravagant
    C. brave
    D. lavish

33. Pique most nearly means:
    A. amuse
    B. enchant
    C. apply
    D. irritate

34. Upheaval most nearly means:
    A. movement
    B. tumult
    C. launch
    D. hoist

35. Indignant most nearly means:
    A. offended
    B. worried
    C. angry
    D. excited

VOCABULARY PRACTICE TEST 5

1. His comments always contain a little bit of sarcasm.
   A. criticism
   B. contempt
   C. bitterness
   D. irony

2. He was lurking at the side of the building.
   A. hiding
   B. waiting
   C. loitering
   D. walking

3. Fraternize most nearly means:
   A. encourage
   B. befriend
   C. support
   D. communicate

4. Disparity most nearly means:
   A. disagreement
   B. disharmony
   C. inequality
   D. impartiality

5. The country's monetary policy is controlled by the government.
   A. interest
   B. investment
   C. foreign
   D. financial

6. The store specializes in various types of apparel.
   A. devices
   B. accessories
   C. clothing
   D. equipment

7. Chimera most nearly means:
   A. fireplace
   B. chimney
   C. setback
   D. illusion

8. Champion most nearly means:
   A. defend
   B. defeat
   C. fight
   D. overthrow

9. She was fettered with many responsibilities.
   A. accompanied
   B. restricted
   C. overjoyed
   D. blessed

10. I have never met a more fickle person.
    A. capricious
    B. fun-loving
    C. determined
    D. reliable

11. Momentous most nearly means:
    A. thought-provoking
    B. short-lived
    C. significant
    D. enormous

12. Perpetual most nearly means the opposite of:
    A. irritating
    B. extensive
    C. continuous
    D. short-lived

13. She is really temperamental in the morning.
    A. grumpy
    B. sleepy
    C. alert
    D. energetic

14. The new law will set a(n) precedent.
    A. system
    B. regulation
    C. exemplar
    D. authority

15. Juvenile most nearly means:
    A. underdeveloped
    B. immature
    C. inexperienced
    D. inexpert

16. Feeble most nearly means:
    A. forgetful
    B. old-age
    C. fake
    D. weak

17. She was commended for her actions.
    A. praised
    B. reported
    C. reprimanded
    D. criticized

18. Ostensibly, he is a nice person.
    A. obviously
    B. seemingly
    C. occasionally
    D. rarely

19. Aloof most nearly means:
    A. lonely
    B. lofty
    C. indifferent
    D. confident

20. Confiscate most nearly means:
    A. claim
    B. seize
    C. inspect
    D. remove

21. We will have to tolerate her behavior.
    A. blame
    B. castigate
    C. welcome
    D. endure

22. They were looking forward to the advent of their boss.
    A. season
    B. celebration
    C. arrival
    D. birth

23. All applicants must undergo a stringent background investigation.
    A. strict
    B. handy
    C. brief
    D. stingy

24. Jeopardy most nearly means:
    A. immunity
    B. exposure
    C. danger
    D. depth

25. Putrid most nearly means:
    A. awful
    B. inedible
    C. smelly
    D. rotten

26. He approaches every task with alacrity.
    A. eagerness
    B. reluctance
    C. reproach
    D. wholesomeness

27. The king abdicated his power.
    A. renewed
    B. relinquished
    C. rejected
    D. reinforced

28. Futile most nearly means:
    A. unnecessary
    B. pointless
    C. fecund
    D. fruitful

29. Inimical most nearly means:
    A. imitated
    B. mocked
    C. adverse
    D. averse

30. Florence Nightingale was undaunted in her work, even in times of crisis.
    A. crucial
    B. decisive
    C. admirable
    D. intrepid

31. The prison officers usually subjugate prisoners who attempt to riot.
    A. discourage
    B. punish
    C. prevent
    D. suppress

32. Reticent most nearly means:
    A. taciturn
    B. humble
    C. ebullient
    D. depressed

33. Unscrupulous most nearly means the opposite of:
    A. frank
    B. honest
    C. corrupt
    D. ruthless

34. Winsome most nearly means:
    A. triumphant
    B. victorious
    C. charming
    D. vanquishing

35. Renovate most nearly means:
    A. restore
    B. demolish
    C. clean up
    D. dispose of

VOCABULARY PRACTICE TEST 6

1. The company has been dormant since 2012.
   A. successful
   B. viable
   C. incorporated
   D. inactive

2. She always has the most ingenious ideas.
   A. benevolent
   B. ridiculous
   C. popular
   D. inventive

3. You will be given more information when the ceremony commences.
   A. concludes
   B. begins
   C. continues
   D. culminates

4. Propensity most nearly means:
   A. enthusiasm
   B. interest
   C. proclivity
   D. competence

5. Domineer most nearly means:
   A. dominate
   B. threaten
   C. submit
   D. surrender

6. The governor decided to show clemency to the prisoners.
   A. justice
   B. mercy
   C. peace
   D. hope

7. He said that we have to abridge the document.
   A. shorten
   B. interpret
   C. mail
   D. file

8. Abyss most nearly means:
   A. infection
   B. inflammation
   C. chasm
   D. valley

9. Pugnacious most nearly means:
   A. fearless
   B. tenacious
   C. vigorous
   D. quarrelsome

10. Of all of the volunteers on the campaign, she has been the most stalwart.
    A. strong
    B. loyal
    C. defensive
    D. resilient

11. The high salary <u>enticed</u> him into accepting the job.
    A. tricked
    B. blackmailed
    C. lured
    D. bribed

12. The accountant determined the <u>cumulative</u> amount of the expenses.
    A. total
    B. excessive
    C. yearly
    D. costly

13. Her job is as president of the college is <u>trying</u>.
    A. demanding
    B. interesting
    C. experimental
    D. boring

14. <u>Trite</u> most nearly means:
    A. wasteful
    B. impure
    C. brief
    D. banal

15. <u>Unscathed</u> most nearly means:
    A. healthy
    B. unharmed
    C. impaired
    D. spoiled

16. <u>Abhorrent</u> most nearly means:
    A. relinquished
    B. ceased
    C. detestable
    D. commendable

17. Her story was full of <u>hyperbole</u>.
    A. enchantment
    B. exhilaration
    C. preoccupation
    D. exaggeration

18. He might find it hard to make friends at college because he is so <u>studious</u>.
    A. bookish
    B. selfish
    C. aloof
    D. serious

19. <u>Transpose</u> most nearly means:
    A. note down
    B. exchange
    C. interpose
    D. interject

20. <u>Respite</u> most nearly means:
    A. inhale
    B. breathe
    C. rest
    D. recuperate

21. <u>Suppress</u> most nearly means the opposite of:
    A. subdue
    B. defeat
    C. control
    D. incite

22. Purge most nearly means:
    A. eliminate
    B. escalate
    C. upsurge
    D. filtrate

23. Opaque most nearly means the opposite of:
    A. obscure
    B. cloudy
    C. darkened
    D. transparent

24. Her taste in clothing is very eccentric.
    A. trendy
    B. stylish
    C. unconventional
    D. distinctive

25. Their relationship is full of acrimony.
    A. sarcasm
    B. disharmony
    C. ambiguity
    D. ambivalence

26. Carrying out their strategy involved intricate planning.
    A. complex
    B. lengthy
    C. manageable
    D. cooperative

27. Precinct most nearly means:
    A. station
    B. office
    C. territory
    D. site

28. Remunerate most nearly means:
    A. advance
    B. reclaim
    C. acquire
    D. compensate

29. Satire most nearly means:
    A. mockery
    B. contempt
    C. ill feeling
    D. practical joke

30. Mulct most nearly means:
    A. deceive
    B. defraud
    C. shred
    D. decompose

31. Disclose most nearly means:
    A. publicize
    B. circulate
    C. unfold
    D. uncover

32. Calamity most nearly means:
    A. threat
    B. danger
    C. disaster
    D. disease

33. Artifact most nearly means:
    A. actuality
    B. certainty
    C. antique
    D. relic

34. Dispatch most nearly means:
    A. send out
    B. go forward
    C. state
    D. communicate

35. Paradigm most nearly means:
    A. order
    B. model
    C. summit
    D. culmination

VOCABULARY PRACTICE TEST 7

1. The villain robbed the bank, killing two people.
   A. prisoner
   B. robber
   C. murderer
   D. outlaw

2. Wayward most nearly means:
   A. purposeless
   B. pointless
   C. contrary
   D. curved

3. We need to consider the consequences of our actions.
   A. success of
   B. motivations for
   C. reasons for
   D. results of

4. Acquiesce most nearly means:
   A. accept
   B. ignore
   C. assimilate
   D. accommodate

5. Ford is a(n) forerunner in the automotive industry.
   A. enterprise
   B. company
   C. leader
   D. giant

6. Patent most nearly means:
   A. showy
   B. visible
   C. obscure
   D. permitted

7. The vacation that they had planned failed to materialize.
   A. be enjoyable
   B. continue
   C. prevail
   D. happen

8. Lenient most nearly means:
   A. easy-going
   B. lazy
   C. improper
   D. insolent

9. They operate a legitimate business activity.
   A. prosperous
   B. profitable
   C. defunct
   D. lawful

10. Dismal most nearly means:
    A. ill-advised
    B. poorly planned
    C. disastrous
    D. erroneous

11. Gossiping about others can actually be quite pernicious.
    A. extensive
    B. damaging
    C. truthful
    D. exciting

12. This machine has a defect which prevents it from functioning.
    A. fault
    B. safety
    C. problem
    D. protection

13. The house was engulfed in flames.
    A. ablaze in
    B. ignited by
    C. incinerated by
    D. overcome by

14. Façade most nearly means:
    A. deface
    B. apparel
    C. appearance
    D. incognito

15. Propitiate most nearly means:
    A. appease
    B. modify
    C. rain
    D. snow

16. Ephemeral most nearly means:
    A. adorned
    B. bejeweled
    C. enduring
    D. short-lived

17. They used several gimmicks to sell their product.
    A. advertisements
    B. promotions
    C. tricks
    D. discounts

18. I really don't think he should dispense advice to you.
    A. offer
    B. give
    C. exclude
    D. dismiss

19. Advocate most nearly means:
    A. judge
    B. proponent
    C. adversary
    D. arbiter

20. Laud most nearly means:
    A. observe
    B. proclaim
    C. honor
    D. bolster

21. The amount he is paid is a pittance.
    A. insufficient
    B. shameful
    C. permitted
    D. illegal

22. He sat by the lake, contemplating his problems.
    A. reviewing
    B. reliving
    C. trying to forget
    D. thinking about

23. This pipe has been galvanized with a special coating.
    A. treated
    B. covered
    C. fabricated
    D. strengthened

24. Dubious most nearly means:
    A. unfavorable
    B. doubtful
    C. undeniable
    D. pessimistic

25. A(n) noxious gas was used in order to eliminate all of the insects.
    A. invisible
    B. innocuous
    C. toxic
    D. luxurious

26. The troops will debouch at the base of the valley.
    A. emerge
    B. camp
    C. disarm
    D. strategize

27. Parity most nearly means:
    A. verity
    B. equality
    C. combine
    D. establish

28. Accord most nearly means:
    A. antagonist
    B. advocate
    C. resemblance
    D. agreement

29. Bequest most nearly means:
    A. appeal
    B. application
    C. inheritance
    D. grant

30. Perturb most nearly means:
    A. annoy
    B. astound
    C. fascinate
    D. stimulate

31. Reproach most nearly means:
    A. access
    B. criticize
    C. prove
    D. rescind

32. Concatenation most nearly means:
    A. noise
    B. disorder
    C. territory
    D. combination

33. Eulogy most nearly means:
    A. speech
    B. tribute
    C. funeral
    D. remembrance

34. Temporal most nearly means:
    A. spiritual
    B. psychological
    C. earthly
    D. ephemeral

35. Vigilant most nearly means:
    A. watchful
    B. restless
    C. defensive
    D. sleepless

VOCABULARY PRACTICE TEST 8

1. He is currently being prosecuted for armed robbery.
   A. suspected of
   B. tried for
   C. committed of
   D. sentenced for

2. Reclusive most nearly means:
   A. gregarious
   B. garrulous
   C. solitary
   D. exceptional

3. Obsequious most nearly means:
   A. decorated
   B. showy
   C. subservient
   D. introverted

4. Anomie most nearly means:
   A. seafood
   B. shellfish
   C. despair
   D. chaos

5. She was usually cynical about other people's motives.
   A. distrustful
   B. sarcastic
   C. reluctant
   D. resisting

6. Extraneous most nearly means:
   A. irreverent
   B. irrelevant
   C. eliminated
   D. obscure

7. Blatant most nearly means:
   A. profuse
   B. vague
   C. flagrant
   D. mysterious

8. Fervid most nearly means:
   A. illuminated
   B. afflicted
   C. nervous
   D. ardent

9. The judge lessened the sentence for the crime due to mitigating circumstances.
   A. extenuating
   B. implicating
   C. incriminating
   D. swindling

10. Defray most nearly means:
    A. tear
    B. bear
    C. exude
    D. intensify

11. Nefarious most nearly means:
    A. foreign
    B. peripheral
    C. wicked
    D. nebulous

12. Liaison most nearly means:
    A. avoidance
    B. clandestine
    C. complication
    D. communication

13. Garrison most nearly means:
    A. fort
    B. barracks
    C. latrine
    D. duty

14. She always seems to have some malady.
    A. complaint
    B. illness
    C. comment
    D. compliment

15. Antecedent most nearly means:
    A. event
    B. precursor
    C. death
    D. consequence

16. Jetty most nearly means:
    A. abandon
    B. overboard
    C. pier
    D. cargo

17. Parking fines are not considered to be serious infringements.
    A. regulations
    B. deterrents
    C. ordinances
    D. offenses

18. Proviso most nearly means:
    A. stipulation
    B. ration
    C. plan
    D. arrangement

19. Turbulent most nearly means:
    A. quiescent
    B. windy
    C. powerful
    D. tumultuous

20. The suspect was exonerated for the crime.
    A. exposed
    B. deliberated
    C. cleared
    D. freed

21. Zest most nearly means:
    A. enthusiasm
    B. strength
    C. courage
    D. ambition

22. Resolute most nearly means:
    A. corrupt
    B. licentious
    C. degenerate
    D. determined

23. Unilateral most nearly means:
    A. approved
    B. accepted
    C. one-sided
    D. universal

24. Vestibule most nearly means:
    A. room
    B. entrance
    C. cloak
    D. coat

25. In the end, my input was incidental.
    A. minor
    B. overlooked
    C. detrimental
    D. significant

26. Servility most nearly means:
    A. hospitality
    B. hostility
    C. abandonment
    D. submissiveness

27. We need to avoid mawkish comments if we are going to remain positive.
    A. defamatory
    B. malicious
    C. maudlin
    D. negative

28. Indispensable most nearly means:
    A. permanent
    B. necessary
    C. stalwart
    D. non-degradable

29. No one could understand the nebulous instructions.
    A. extensive
    B. unclear
    C. verbose
    D. complicated

30. Subterfuge most nearly means:
    A. trickery
    B. artillery
    C. bombardment
    D. vicissitude

31. Pending most nearly means:
    A. low hanging
    B. ventilated
    C. impervious
    D. undecided

32. Obsolete most nearly means:
    A. superfluous
    B. perfunctory
    C. broken
    D. outdated

33. We need to rectify a few items on the report.
    A. change
    B. comment on
    C. correct
    D. clarify

34. Sycophant most nearly means:
    A. musician
    B. flatterer
    C. complainer
    D. superior

35. Vindictive most nearly means:
    A. revengeful
    B. conquering
    C. domineering
    D. malcontent

ANSWERS TO THE BONUS EXERCISES

Test 1:

1) B
2) C
3) A
4) D
5) B
6) D
7) A
8) C
9) B
10) D
11) D
12) A
13) B
14) C
15) D
16) A
17) B
18) C
19) B
20) D
21) A
22) D
23) C

24) B

25) D

26) A

27) C

28) D

29) B

30) A

31) C

32) B

33) D

34) A

35) C

Test 2:

1) C

2) A

3) D

4) D

5) B

6) D

7) A

8) B

9) C

10) D

11) A

12) B

13) D

14) C

15) A

16) A

17) B

18) D

19) C

20) B

21) A

22) D

23) C

24) B

25) A

26) A

27) B

28) C

29) D

30) D

31) D

32) B

33) C

34) C

35) D

Test 3:

1) B
2) C
3) A
4) D
5) D
6) A
7) B
8) C
9) D
10) A
11) B
12) A
13) D
14) B
15) B
16) A
17) C
18) A
19) D
20) B
21) B
22) C
23) C
24) A

25) D

26) B

27) D

28) C

29) A

30) B

31) D

32) A

33) C

34) B

35) D

Test 4:

1) C

2) A

3) B

4) D

5) C

6) B

7) C

8) A

9) D

10) C

11) B

12) A

13) B

14) D

15) C

16) C

17) B

18) A

19) D

20) C

21) A

22) B

23) D

24) C

25) D

26) B

27) A

28) A

29) C

30) D

31) B

32) C

33) D

34) B

35) A

Test 5:

1) D
2) A
3) B
4) C
5) D
6) C
7) D
8) A
9) B
10) A
11) C
12) D
13) A
14) C
15) B
16) D
17) A
18) B
19) C
20) B
21) D
22) C
23) A
24) C

25) D

26) A

27) B

28) B

29) C

30) D

31) D

32) A

33) B

34) C

35) A

Test 6:

1) D

2) D

3) B

4) C

5) A

6) B

7) A

8) C

9) D

10) B

11) C

12) A

13) A

14) D

15) B

16) C

17) D

18) A

19) B

20) C

21) D

22) A

23) D

24) C

25) B

26) A

27) C

28) D

29) A

30) B

31) D

32) C

33) D

34) A

35) B

Test 7:

1) D
2) C
3) D
4) A
5) C
6) B
7) D
8) A
9) D
10) C
11) B
12) A
13) D
14) C
15) A
16) D
17) C
18) B
19) B
20) C
21) A
22) D
23) D
24) B

25) C

26) A

27) B

28) D

29) C

30) A

31) B

32) D

33) B

34) C

35) A

Test 8:

1) B

2) C

3) C

4) D

5) A

6) B

7) C

8) D

9) A

10) B

11) C

12) D

13) A

14) B

15) B

16) C

17) D

18) A

19) D

20) C

21) A

22) D

23) C

24) B

25) A

26) D

27) C

28) B

29) B

30) A

31) D

32) D

33) C

34) B

35) A